The Price of Economic Freedom:
A Guide to Flexible Rates

By the same author

Steering the Economy: The Role of the Treasury
Left or Right: The Bogus Dilemma

The Price of Economic Freedom

A Guide to Flexible Rates

SAMUEL BRITTAN

Macmillan

St Martin's Press

First published 1970 by
MACMILLAN AND CO LTD
London and Basingstoke
Associated companies in New York Toronto
Dublin Melbourne Johannesburg and Madras

SBN 333 11706 9

Library of Congress catalog card no. 73-130745

Printed in Great Britain by
R. & R. CLARK LTD
Edinburgh

Contents

List of Illustrations

There still prevails, even in nations well acquainted with commerce, a strong jealousy with regard to the balance of trade, and a fear that all their gold and silver may be leaving them.

David Hume, *Of The Balance of Trade* (1742)

Introduction: The Balance of Payments Myth

During the whole of the last decade the nation was exhorted by politicians, television programmes and many very worthy bodies to accept two beliefs: (*a*) that the balance of payments was the biggest industrial, economic, political and even moral problem the nation faced, and (*b*) that it was the personal responsibility of every citizen. A moralistic approach to economics prevailed in which specialised commentators were asked on television if people could feel less guilty when the trade figures improved. There were documentary films, business conferences, books, pamphlets and poster campaigns emphasising the sinister threat of national bankruptcy, and our individual duty to work harder to prevent it. Some of these – to the embarrassment of their authors – saw the light of the day in the early months of 1970 when the British balance of payments had, according to the official figures, never been 'better'. Even then the syndrome did not disappear, and the most serious statesmen, diplomats and even official economists believed that the biggest obstacle to Britain joining the E.E.C. was the balance of payments cost.

This book has three main objects. The first is to explain why the balance of payments is a *pseudo-problem*, artificially created by the attempt to freeze exchange rates and/or mistaken domestic financial management. But like all self-created problems, it is capable of doing untold harm if allowed to persist. If exchange rates were flexible, as advocated in the following pages, there is a very high probability that the balance of payments would be relegated to a very minor place among policy questions for any country that conducted its affairs with reasonable – not ideal – prudence.

The years of passing the begging bowl around the I.M.F. and central bankers, and the imaginary picture of national poverty conjured up for so long, were, I shall argue, quite unnecessary. Yet if we attempt to stick to a rigid exchange rate these events could all too easily recur. Nothing would be more foolhardy than to predict what the balance of payments will be when this book appears in the reader's hand. The only certainty is that under a fixed exchange rate it can change with lightning rapidity. This book is going to press in Spring 1970, at a time when on almost any definition Britain has a larger surplus than any country in Europe or North America. Yet only nine months previously the world's financial statesmen were alarmed at the persistence of an apparently incurable British deficit, and the letters of the Greek alphabet were nearly exhausted in devising contingency plans for different types of emergency.

Thus, however good the balance of payments figures for 1970 appear, it is far too early to say that the pseudo-problem of the balance of payments is a matter of history. (Nor should one forget that there would also be troubles and embarrassments of a less familiar kind if a fixed exchange rate were to lead to a large and continuing surplus.) It is important to expose all the recent propaganda which saw the balance of payments as a battle for national survival as the confidence trick that it was, if we are to avoid being taken in on future occasions.

This basic argument, which occupies the first part of the book, should be of interest to anyone who has followed British politics and the way it has been dominated by mysterious payments crises and equally mysterious periods of apparent recovery. The second aim of this work is to outline in a little more detail in Part II the positive case for flexible exchange rates and in particular to discuss the objections raised by those who are sceptical of the idea. The 'question and answer' approach adopted here (as well as in some pages of Part I) is for the reader's convenience and is not intended to convey an impression of omniscience. Part II covers both floating exchange rates, in which the price of a currency would be determined by supply and demand in the market place, and compromise plans for limited flexibility under which exchange rates would change more easily and more gradually than under the present system. There is some discussion of what is probable as well as of what is desirable (pp. 88–9) and Chapter 8 includes a discussion of the effects of joining the E.E.C. Although written from a definite point of view, I hope that this book will elucidate and inform, as well as persuade. For its third purpose is to provide an outline guide to the basic economics of exchange rates, reserves and the balance of payments, which will be useful even to those who do not go along with all the policy conclusions.

It is best to explain at the outset in what sense the balance of payments is a pseudo-problem. Examples of real problems include the pressure of population on limited land in the South-East, bad industrial relations, or an unsatisfactory productivity performance. These cannot be tackled by a uniform alteration in any set of numbers. If wages and prices were half or twice of what they are, or if the pound were devalued to $1.40 or revalued to $4.80, there would still be no more land in the South-East, industrial troubles would not change their nature, and the underlying level of productivity would be no different. The balance of payments is on the other hand a pseudo-problem because its nature and size is an arbitrary one depending on artificial ratios of this kind. A change in international exchange rates or in the ratio of money wages at home and abroad, unconnected with any fundamental change in performance, can transform a vast surplus into a tremendous deficit, or vice versa. To talk of battles for national survival and invoke Dunkirk in such situations is bogus patriotism, which creates quite unnecessary guilt-feelings in those who take official propaganda seriously, and vague and unhelpful anxieties in others.

One of the oldest and most effective debating tricks is to accuse the other person of 'offering a panacea'. Applied to flexible exchange rates, such a charge would be peculiarly inappropriate. Real incomes and living standards depend on the efficiency with which we use our resources. Under no system can the inhabitants of a country have more goods and services than they can earn, or borrow from overseas. Under no system can demand run ahead of productive capacity without the excess being cancelled out by higher prices. If the pseudo-problem of 'earning foreign exchange' were to be removed, the real economic problems of using limited resources to best advantage would occupy the centre of the stage. Admittedly some of these real problems now appear disguised as balance of payments difficulties. But when they appear in this distorted form their true nature is hidden from sight, and the wrong remedies are likely to be adopted.

How to use our resources to best advantage is a controversial question, but one on which we are free to make our own decisions. Mr E. J. Mishan is quite right to explode the myth that we need to keep up with the Americans or Europeans in a supposed technological race or go under as a nation. These things are certainly a matter of choice, and we can if we wish opt for a quieter life, and more leisure without supersonic aircraft or a 'home-based computer industry'.[1] Such a choice may or may not be desirable, and one may think that Mr Mishan carries his scepticism about growth and productivity too far. A great deal of the social case against productivity improvement is really a case against crude methods of measurement which do not take the destruction of amenity into account. But the arguments should be considered on their own merits without imagining that our choices are constrained by a balance of payments straitjacket. The straitjacket is entirely self-imposed and we can throw it off whenever we choose.

There can be little rational doubt about the harmful illogicality of making the saving and earning of foreign exchange the main feature of our economic and foreign policy and of our business morality. The particular virtue of foreign exchange would disappear if the pound were correctly valued in relation to other currencies and were expected to remain correctly valued in future. The area where reasonable men can differ is in the merits and difficulties of the alternative ways of keeping exchange rates in the right relation to each other. The nineteenth-century gold standard was one such way, and a world currency would be another. But even if it were desirable to do so, it would be even more difficult to reinstate the one or inaugurate the other than to make exchange rates flexible. I have, however, had no hesitation in discussing the difficulties and uncertainties in the case for various kinds of flexibility. It is a common logical error to examine the strengths and defects of a single system in isolation. No proposal, whether for flexible rates, or increasing the price of gold, reforming NATO, leaving Vietnam or establishing comprehensive schools, can be meaningfully judged except in relation to the alternatives. There are weaknesses in every system, and the real question is whether the probable drawbacks of more flexible exchange rates exceed the drawbacks of the present supposedly fixed system – and similarly with the advantages.

The subject of fixed versus flexible exchange rates has already been extensively discussed in many excellent books, articles and papers. My main excuse for writing about it again is the amount of strong feeling, misconception and puzzlement which this subject still arouses. The deleterious effect of so-called 'fixed exchange rates' extends to large areas of public life, well beyond the strictly economic. It therefore seems worth trying to find out if the approach of an economic journalist can throw any light on the subject. Any intellectual novelty is confined to the 'question and answer' approach in certain sections, the discussion of some of the broader implications of the subject and the linking of the general case to actual British experience. There is inevitably some overlapping with previous works by other authors, to whom my indebtedness is great. To have eliminated this would have been to sacrifice all hope of clarity for the sake of product differentiation. But for a full statement of the theory of exchange rates, or for the historical record, the reader is referred to the existing literature.[2]

The division of this book into two parts, the first designed for the general reader interested in public affairs and the second for those with a special interest in economic policy, and the 'question and answer' approach, have drawbacks as well as advantages. The chief drawback is that the first reference to a topic is often separated by a good many pages from its elaboration and the discussion of any complications. It might repay the critical reader to turn over a few more pages before exclaiming, 'He hasn't dealt with X' or 'How about the Y problem?'. Judgment is of course involved in deciding what is the heart of the matter and what is a complication or elaboration, and for this I must take full responsibility.

Finally, and on a more personal level, I am extremely grateful to Mr Ronald Grierson, Professor Harry Johnson, Mr A. J. W. S. Leonard, Mr David Lomax, Mr Christopher McMahon and Professor John Williamson for reading at short notice a preliminary version of the manuscript and providing the kind of helpful and detailed comments that authors badly need and so rarely receive. Mr John Cooper gave me helpful advice on forward markets. The Bank of England was extremely helpful on a technical point. Jock Bruce-Gardyne, Ian Davidson and Kelsey van Musschenbroek supplied me with the critical questions which triggered off the whole enterprise. Unfortunately none of the individuals mentioned – and still less the organisations with which they are associated – is necessarily committed to the views expressed.

This book went to press before the second 'temporary' floating of the Canadian dollar at the beginning of June, 1970.

PART ONE

The Self-Inflicted Straitjacket

1 The Present System

Most countries have a 'par value' for their currencies. This is the official rate of exchange, notified to the International Monetary Fund. Par values are expressed in terms of gold as well as of the U.S. dollar. A few currencies such as the French, Swiss and Belgian francs are legally defined in domestic legislation in terms of gold. But these legal fictions are misleading. In no major industrial country does the central bank or government supply gold to currency holders on demand, as was generally the case before 1914.

The U.S.A. is a partial exception, as *overseas* holders of *official dollar balances* have the theoretical right to convert them into gold at $35 per fine ounce for 'legitimate monetary purposes' – a concept that has never been satisfactorily defined. The U.S.A. will certainly buy gold from other countries, but would today be most unlikely to agree to sell very large sums to them, now that its official gold stock has fallen towards the $10,000 million level; and the major dollar-holding countries have tried to avoid putting the Americans to the test.

It is the exchange rate against the dollar that matters for practical purposes. National authorities intervene in the foreign exchange market to prevent the rate against the dollar going outside specified, and narrow, limits. The result is that all the currencies in the system are thereby virtually fixed against each other. The I.M.F. rules permit a variation of 1 per cent on either side of the *par value*. The official British limits, at the time of writing, of $2.38 to $2.42, thus take advantage of nearly, but not quite all, the permitted range of variation.

Left to the market, exchange rates would settle every day at a level where the demand for each currency balanced the supply. A surplus of sterling, whether due to a basic payments deficit or short-term movements of funds, would lead to an automatic fall in the rate until it reached a level where it seemed once more an attractive bargain and buyers came in to support it. A deficiency of sterling at the prevailing rate would by a similar process lead to an appreciation.

Under the present system, the Bank of England is committed to buy sterling to prevent the pound falling below $2.38. To do so it has to pay out dollars. Conversely it sells sterling for dollars if the rate should threaten to break through the $2.42 ceiling. The Bank may also intervene, when convenient, in currencies other than dollars. But its operations, like those of other central banks, are most frequently in dollars, and these are all that are strictly necessary. For this reason the dollar is known as the *intervention currency*.

It is by means of such intervention in the foreign exchange market that *reserves* are normally lost or gained. Between the two limits the Bank of England can act at its discretion. But the margin between them is so small that any large imbalance has to be reflected in the reserves (or in official borrowing from, or repayments to, other countries). The published movement of the sterling exchange rate means very little without a knowledge of official tactics, which are normally a closely guarded secret. The interesting question is not how far the rate has moved in any period, but how much foreign exchange the Bank of England has paid out or taken in to prevent the movement going even further.

Although fixed for long periods at a time, the central par value of a currency is liable to occasional change under the I.M.F. rules in the case of 'fundamental disequilibrium'. This system is usually known as the *adjustable peg*, *par value*, *normally fixed exchange rates* or *Bretton Woods* system (named after the place in the U.S.A. where the I.M.F. Agreement was drafted in 1944). In practice parity changes have only been made as a matter of last resort, and have taken place in fair-sized jumps, especially in the case of devaluation (e.g. the 14·3 per cent sterling devaluation of 1967). For this reason the system has also been aptly labelled by Professor Harry Johnson one of *reluctant adjustment*.[3]

If they are to prevent the price of their currencies from straying outside their official limits, national authorities need reserves of foreign exchange which they can use to intervene in the foreign exchange market. As already mentioned, the dollar is the main currency used for this purpose. Most countries have, however, liked to maintain a large gold component in their reserves. They have been able to use their gold holdings to buy any foreign exchange they need from the U.S. or other national authorities (although since March 1968 they have agreed not to make such purchases from the private market).

Apart from gold and dollars, sterling has been used for reserves by Sterling Area countries, but such sterling holdings amount to a modest and diminishing proportion of total world reserves – about 8 per cent of the total in the spring of 1970. Countries have been able to offset drains on their reserves by temporary drawings from the I.M.F. or from other central banks via the 'Basle' network. But such drawings had to be repaid and were only available in times of difficulty. On 1 January 1970 the I.M.F. took a big stride forward by distributing the first allocation of *Special Drawing Rights* (S.D.R.s). The great innovation is that S.D.R.s are new paper assets deliberately created to supplement existing world reserves – hence their popular name 'paper gold'. They are distributed to all I.M.F. members, as of right, and count as part of members' owned reserves. They thus provide another way – apart from intervention in the foreign exchange market when their own currencies are in demand, or by gold mining – by which national authorities can gain modest amounts of reserves each year. The initial world allocation of S.D.R.s amounts to $3,500 million for 1970 and $3,000 million in each of the subsequent years 1971 and 1972. Britain's allocation in 1970 was £171 million and will come to approximately £140 million in the two subsequent years.

Unlike foreign exchange (or gold in countries where private holdings are permitted) S.D.R.s can only be held by national or international monetary authorities, who can use them according to agreed rules to obtain currencies from each other. The new device should do something to alleviate the threat of a world shortage of reserves. But neither S.D.R.s, nor access to international credits, can do more than buy time for a country such as Britain if there is a sizeable imbalance between the supply and demand for sterling at the current exchange rate. The question of how to tackle such imbalances, usually labelled the *international adjustment problem*, is important for both Britain and for the world's financial system. Numerous alternatives have been suggested to the present system of changing exchange rates, some of which have been under examination by the I.M.F. since its annual meeting in 1969.

2 Other Systems

Unfortunately there is no agreed terminology for alternative currency systems. One can therefore only hope to separate concepts; the words used to describe them differ slightly from one writer to another.

One could imagine *immutable* or *rigid* exchange rates, which were not subject to change at all. These would prevail automatically if a *commodity money* such as gold provided the only domestic money in all countries, or if there were one international paper currency. (It would not matter if this currency circulated under different names in different countries, provided that people were confident that these pieces of paper were mutually convertible at immutable rates for the indefinite future.) In practice rigidity is a matter of degree. Even in the heyday of the gold standard, countries suspended gold convertibility and went on to paper standards in times of crisis, and it is possible to imagine Home Rule circumstances in which Scottish pound notes might circulate at a discount or premium over English ones.

One limited change in the present system would be a *widening of the margins* around the official parity, and at the 1969 I.M.F. meeting Mr Jenkins did propose a widening to 2 per cent on either side of the official par value. But the central point would not itself vary under his proposals.

A more fundamental reform would be for one or more countries to adopt a *floating rate*. There would be no official parity and rates would be determined by supply and demand in the foreign exchange market. The authorities might still intervene in an attempt to iron out fluctuations. A system in which they stayed out completely, and left the rate entirely to the market, might be called *freely fluctuating rates*.

There is also a whole family of compromises (to be discussed later in this book) which would retain a central official parity, but allow that parity to move gradually upwards or downwards by small amounts – of perhaps up to 2 or 3 per cent – in the course of each year. Such schemes are known by a confusing number of near synonyms such as the *moving rate*, *slowly moving rate*, *moving band*, *sliding parity*, *gliding parity*, *mobile parity*, or (hideously) *crawling peg*. They are advocated in two main varieties, the 'market' and 'discretionary' versions. Under the 'discretionary' version the authorities would have the option of announcing small shifts in the central parity at frequent intervals. Suggestions here have ranged from weekly to monthly or quarterly determinations. The more frequent the changes, the smaller, of course, would be the permissible amount. A discretionary moving parity could of course be combined with wider margins, but need not be. Under the 'market' version of the moving parity the official parity would be the average of market rates over a given period, say the past year. (The limit to the possible movement would be set by the permitted margin by which the market rate could deviate from the parity at any one time, and thus affect the average.)

Innumerable other hybrids and compromises are possible, a few of which are listed in Table 1 below. Clearly the distinction between fixed and flexible rates is one of degree. The following table shows the distinction which is made for the purposes of this book.

Table 1

GUIDE TO EXCHANGE RATE SYSTEMS

1. *Genuinely fixed exchange rates*
   Such a system would include:
   (*a*) The old gold standard.
   (*b*) A world currency.
2. *So-called 'fixed exchange rates', known to be liable to change*
   (*a*) The 'adjustable peg' as practised under the present 'Bretton Woods' system.
   (*b*) Any small widening of the margins under this system which does not allow the central parity to move.
3. *Flexible systems*

(*a*) Freely fluctuating rates. (*b*) Floating rates with some official intervention.	'Floating exchange rates'
(*c*) All varieties of slowly moving parity. (*d*) Sufficiently frequent and small changes in an 'adjustable peg' to approximate to (*c*) above. (*e*) Normally fixed rates, but willingness of governments to resort to periods of floating at early sign of disequilibrium before fixing new parity.	'Compromise forms of flexibility'

Clearly the division could be drawn in a number of different places. The reason for defining flexible rates in this book in the broad manner of section 3 of the above table is that all the variants listed as 'flexible' would:

(*a*) allow exchange rate changes to be used as *a normal* method of international adjustment rather than as a last resort (they could therefore be used early *rather than late*); and

(*b*) allow adjustments to be either *gradual and continuous*, or at least to be taken in *frequent small steps* rather than in sudden jumps.

Despite the strong case that can be made for fully floating rates, this book is not primarily concerned to advocate any one particular form of flexibility, but to explain the harmful effects of the present system of so-called 'fixed rates' and the need to make some change. Perhaps I should add that there is a case to be made for genuinely fixed rates which (short of wars or similar calamities) commanded perfect confidence. It would not be my first choice in the present state of the world economy, and in any case it is almost inconceivable in a world of paper currencies which lacks an international political authority. But the point that will occur again and again, and especially in Chapter 7, is that genuinely fixed rates under (1) in the above table, and flexible rates under (3), have more in common with each other than either has with the present supposedly 'fixed rate' system listed under (2). The present system gives neither the stability of really fixed rates, nor the independence of internal policy of flexible systems. It does on the other hand manufacture balance of payments problems and currency crises on a scale peculiarly its own.

3 Exchange Rates and the Balance of Payments

Let us start with a country with a given level of costs and prices, relative to those of other countries, and a given level of industrial management and labour relations, salesmanship and design, attractiveness to foreign investors, and all the other elements that make up its competitive position. It also has a government with certain policies, including domestic financial policy, which may or may not inspire confidence at home and abroad. All these, and countless other factors, will determine the demand for and supply of its currency. The price of the currency in terms of foreign currency is the rate of exchange, and there will be a particular rate at which demand and supply will balance.

This simple statement is the basis of all international monetary policy. The rest is commentary based, as Hume remarked, 'on very uncertain facts and suppositions'. The first piece of commentary is that the exchange rate at which demand and supply for a currency will balance depends vitally on the domestic financial policies which the country is pursuing. If domestic demand is high in relation to capacity, or rising rapidly, the exchange rate will be lower than if demand is low, or is rising slowly.

Some internal financial policies can, however, be ruled out from the beginning as undesirable because they are too inflationary in their effects on prices, and others because they are too deflationary and liable to hit production and employment. There may be fierce argument about the range of acceptable demand policies, but it is clearly not unlimited. Combined with every policy within this range, there will be a rate of exchange which will produce a balance in the foreign exchange market.

The relative usefulness of fiscal and monetary policy are outside the scope of the present discussion and the controversy is avoided as far as possible. Whatever the instruments used, financial policy will normally affect both the demand for and supply of a country's currency and the home economy, although sometimes in different proportions. We live in a world of trade union and other institutional forces strongly resistant to downward movements in money earnings, or even to reductions in their rate of increase; but it is also a world where – happily for the general welfare – surplus countries are not indifferent to their rate of inflation. Under the present 'fixed exchange rate' regime, some countries will therefore find themselves in a position where no internal demand management policy which seeks to avoid recession and high unemployment will be sufficient to reverse a deficit in a period of time acceptable to their creditors and their own sense of prudence and self-respect.

The effects of alternative demand management policies on employment, growth and the balance of payments are discussed in more detail in the Appendix. The main point is that if the Government wishes to prevent the market value of its currency from diverging from the official exchange rate without changing the latter, its best course would be to take deflationary action at the first sign of an incipient deficit. If it waits until costs and prices are already out of line with the requirements of the existing parity, deflationary action will have to be more severe, and will be more likely to hit output and employment for a longer period, than if action had been taken earlier. Under the present 'Bretton Woods' system the generous provision of I.M.F. and central bank credits, coupled with the knowledge that 'in the last resort we can devalue', removes the pressure on deficit countries to take corrective action at an early stage. But as governments are understandably reluctant to create slumps and unemployment, and devaluation is still considered a last resort, there are inevitably long periods during which the official exchange rate diverges from its market rate. (Surplus countries that do not wish to inflate will run into imbalances of an opposite kind.)

An attempt to enforce a price different from the market price in any commodity will lead to an endless series of self-created problems. If the price of wheat is fixed above market levels there will be the problems – so well known in the U.S.A. and the E.E.C. – of acreage controls, persuading farmers to plough up good land, the attempted evasion of these controls, expensive storage facilities and the cost to the taxpayer of buying up the surplus wheat and dumping it abroad at a loss.

The price need only be a little too high or too low for these vast difficulties to accumulate. Many people will then be sure that they reflect something more profound than the official price being slightly out of line with the market price; and indeed if the wrong prices are enforced for a sufficient time, the problem does become profound. For if the adjustment is delayed long enough, and the discrepancy between the market-clearing and the fixed price becomes too large, a structural problem can be artificially created. The *sudden withdrawal* of, say, price support for wheat might well lead to bankruptcies, distress and a much more rapid exodus from the land than if the adjustment to market forces had been gradual and continuous. Similarly, the sudden decontrol of all house rents after decades of restriction would produce real hardship for some people. Yet it is the controls that have created the housing shortage and an inadequate stock of rentable accommodation in certain areas.

Of course money has certain special features, which other commodities such as wheat, bananas or housing accommodation do not possess. The exchange rate for a currency affects the whole of a country's dealings with the outside world and therefore the prices of nearly all other commodities, whether directly or indirectly. It is just these special features which make the persistence of a false price more rather than less harmful than would be the case for an individual commodity. If the price of the national currency is wrong, all the hundreds of thousands of specific markets will no longer be able to fulfil their functions, and governments will be tempted to intervene with one – usually vain – intervention after another, to make up for the central distortion.

A country's balance of payments depends on the accident of where it stands in the world pattern of exchange rates and money costs. If a country's exchange rate happens to be too high, it will have a deficit. Even if there is no change either in its efficiency, or in any fundamental factor, the deficit can become a surplus simply because prices start rising faster abroad than at home. The deficit can also become a surplus after a devaluation of its own currency or appreciation by other countries – again with nothing 'fundamental' happening.

The above argument should not be misunderstood. If a country is already enjoying full employment and running a £500 million deficit and has – in order to repay past debits – to shift into surplus, the spending of its own citizens will have for a time to drop, or at least increase less than usual. This is a real sacrifice with nothing 'pseudo' about it. The pseudo-elements arise in two ways. First, the country concerned has not reached this position because of tea-breaks, strikes, bad managements, unimaginative salesmanship or all the other factors about which Ministers preach. None of these bad habits would have produced the deficit if the demand management at home and the exchange rate had been appropriate.

The second pseudo-element arises when a deficit has already occurred. If the country concerned now stops supporting an overvalued exchange rate, the shift to surplus can be accomplished by demand management alone, without export drives, incomes policy, 'Back Britain' drives, travel allowances, consultations with industry, knighthoods for exporters and all the other pressures to persuade citizens into courses of action which it does not really pay them to adopt. If these measures persist, it is a sign that the authorities fear that the exchange rate is still out of line or may become so again.

4 The Current British Situation

The pound was devalued in 1967; this has since been followed by a mark revaluation, and there have been substantial price increases in both the U.S.A. and the Continent of Europe. As a result of these changes the pound was surely not overvalued any more at the beginning of 1970. Once the British authorities took effective action on both the fiscal and monetary fields, the balance of payments improved and it seems likely for most of 1970, at least, to be in pretty large surplus. Why not abjure risky experiments with the exchange rate and concentrate on internal policies to safeguard the present improvement?

Ministers and officials are inevitably concerned with the next few months, or at most the next year or two. This makes it all the more important for others to adopt a longer-term perspective. This does not mean attempting impossible feats of crystal-gazing, but keeping an eye open for the temporary or unusual features of the immediate situation and for forces that might disturb it in the years ahead.

The statistical balance of payments in a particular year is highly misleading. The real test whether we are paying our way is the balance of payments over the whole of an economic cycle. (These have recently been of four- or five-year duration; the present cycle may be rather longer because of devaluation.) Paying our way involves in the British context a surplus rather than a bare balance, not only because of the needs of debt repayment, but also to finance the net extension of export credit, now running at around £300 million per annum, as well as to meet the foreign exchange costs of possible E.E.C. membership. (The return flow of funds following the recovery of confidence in late 1969 was a multiple of the surplus itself, which is defined to cover only current trading and long-term investment flows. To recover funds which were withdrawn in the crises of 1964–7 is one thing. But to rely on a continuing inflow of highly volatile short-term funds for the needs of the next few years would be foolhardy in the extreme, as past experience should surely have taught us.)

In any assessment of the prospects one must look both at immediate distortions and at more fundamental changes likely to affect the underlying trend. On the first count, one cannot avoid observing that during a large part of 1969–70 the balance of payments was benefiting from quite unusually favourable circumstances. In 1969 imports were held back by a combination of prior deposits, an abnormally severe squeeze on credit, import deposits and a rate of domestic growth of only 1½ per cent per annum, or half the long-run trend. Exports were still benefiting from the devaluation stimulus. The remarkably rapid rise in world trade probably deserves less emphasis, as it pushed up the prices of primary products which Britain has to import.

In 1970 it looks as if the U.S. recession will affect British exports. The latter should on the other hand benefit from the boom and resulting pressures on capacity in Continental Europe which seem likely to continue for the first part of the year at least, as well as from German revaluation. On the other hand the slowdown in world industrial production is likely to prevent the prices of Britain's imports from rising at their normal rate and may even cause them to decline. Nevertheless, the primary producing countries – on whose markets Britain is more dependent than most other industrial countries – began the year well cushioned against price falls, with their reserves at an exceptionally high level, and among these countries a disproportionate share of the reserve gain had gone to Sterling Area members.

A moment's reflection on these favourable forces shows that they are by their very nature likely to be temporary. The key question in relation to the $2.40 exchange rate is whether it would enable us to pay our way in a 'normal' year when home output is growing at its trend rate, when the pressure of domestic demand on resources is at an average level, when stockbuilding is normal, when world trade is growing at its long-run rate and when there are no other special factors in either direction. Another key condition is that there should be no emergency controls which we have pledged to abolish, such as the import deposits in the 1968 crisis. Although no year is ever likely to be normal, the concept of a normal year is vital if we are to avoid being mesmerised by the good or bad luck of the most recent set of figures. Indeed, we shall only be in full equilibrium and the exchange rate be right if we can be in balance in a normal year without the aid of policies, such as overseas investment controls, or special government favours to export-earners or import-savers, which owe their sole justification to balance of payments fears.

My own guess – and it can only be a guess – is that at the beginning of 1970 the underlying balance of payments, after allowing for all favourable factors, would have been good enough to sustain the $2.40 exchange rate without special official protection. This brings one to the second and more interesting question about the forces likely to affect this underlying balance in the early and middle 1970s.

Head of the list of favourable factors are the sterling and mark parity changes, which enable us to start off from a much better competitive position than during most of the 1960s. The levelling-out of government overseas spending, which rose sharply in the decade up to 1967, will also be of great importance – provided there are not too many expensive reversals of the East of Suez policy. Another helpful element – at least in the next few years – is the encouragement of British public corporations to raise loan capital overseas, and of companies to finance some of their overseas investment in the same way. Here too, however, the durability of the policy shift cannot be taken for granted. The increased willingness to tolerate less than brimful employment and to keep the money supply in check will also help the balance of payments – if these policies survive the departure of the I.M.F. invigilators after the last drawing on the Fund standby in March 1970.

There are, however, plenty of forces which we can see acting in the opposite direction. Historically British export prices have tended to rise by about 1 per cent faster than our main competitors', and if this trend reasserts itself, the devaluation advantage will be eroded. There is moreover some, admittedly inconclusive, evidence that even under comparable price and profitability conditions, British exporters have tended to do less well than their competitors for all the usual reasons of inadequate salesmanship, servicing and so on.

After the defeat of its attempted union reforms in the summer of 1969 and with the election on the horizon, the Labour Government followed a policy of appeasement on the labour front. The net result was an anti-incomes policy in which government action actually pushed up the rate of increase of wages above that which would have prevailed under the influence of market forces.[4] It is too early at the time of writing to be sure how the ensuing 'wage explosion' has affected the comparison between British labour costs and those of other countries. But a level of money earnings running at 10–12 per cent above that of a year ago does suggest that the devaluation advantage is being gradually undermined. The effect on Britain's balance of payments could take longer to show up, but in the end be more severe, than is generally imagined. A point to bear in mind is that wages and prices probably respond more slowly and to a smaller extent to a 'touch of the brake' in the U.K. than in many competitor countries.

Apart from the wage explosion itself, there are other influences on the horizon likely to raise British costs and prices. An official calculation suggests that the move to equal pay for women will add 3½ per cent to wage bills by 1975. The move to wage-related pensions, whether by the Crossman state scheme or by alternative Conservative measures to expand private provision, will also add to labour costs. A shift to indirect taxation, whether or not involving a value-added tax, will in the first place affect the internal price level. But wages – and therefore export costs – are responsive to cost-of-living changes in any given state of the labour market.

Then there is the balance of payments cost of joining the E.E.C., for which Whitehall itself has given the extremely wide range of £100–£1,100 million. If and when the negotiations succeed and the terms are known, there will still be a large element of uncertainty about the net result. When calculating the balance of payments effect at a fixed parity, one has to take into account not merely the obvious net payments across the exchanges resulting from membership, but also the secondary effects of dearer food on wages and export prices. Some of these secondary effects would also materialise if, even outside the E.E.C., a future Government were to switch the emphasis of farm support from deficiency payments to levies. This is after all announced Conservative policy, and it would not be unknown for a Labour Government to adopt economic ideas first made fashionable in Conservative circles.

How does one weigh up these opposing forces, together with countless other influences on the balance of payments, some of which are bound to come as complete surprises?

It would be better to avoid doing so. A difference of 1 per cent either way, in an overseas turnover of £12,000 million in each direction, can over a five-year cycle make all the difference between a comfortable surplus and a 'fundamental disequilibrium' leading to yet another devaluation. Yet unforeseeable variations in the rate of Continental inflation, in the growth of world trade, military events abroad, international fashion in consumer goods, the effects of North Sea gas on fuel imports, the relative cunning of Volkswagen and B.M.H. car designers, and thousands of other factors, can swing the balance one way or the other. It is therefore hardly surprising that the record of balance of payments predictions, short or long term, is of one embarrassing mistake after another, which only serves to discredit economic forecasts in other areas where they are of value.

The one certainty here is uncertainty. The only worth-while strategy is one that does not depend on a predictive ability which is not at our disposal. If this is admitted, it follows that the risk of the $2.40 exchange rate becoming overvalued in the 1970s is sufficiently great that no responsible policy-maker should leave it out of account, however good the balance of payments figures at any moment in time. The chance of sterling becoming undervalued, as the mark was in the 1960s, cannot be totally neglected, and this would not be nearly as easy to deal with under a fixed parity as is fondly imagined at present. But it will probably try the reader's patience less if the argument concentrates on the more likely overvaluation possibility.

Surely, we ought to run our financial policy so as to prevent the pound from becoming overvalued again. But if we fail, we have surely learned our lesson and will not insist on holding on too long to an overvalued exchange rate?

This is a matter of judgment. The inhibition against a fixed-rate devaluation could be at least as great in the 1970s as in the 1960s. Both political parties went out of their way to proclaim the 1967 devaluation as a 'defeat'. Owing to the miseducation provided by the politicians and the mass media, the difficulties and sacrifices of the ensuing years were regarded as due to the act of devaluation rather than the fact of deficit. Labour, if re-elected, will wish to avoid the permanent label of the Devaluation Party, while the Conservatives, if they win, will be anxious not to be tarred with the same brush.

Would it not be easier for Britain to adjust its exchange rate if the Bretton Woods system were operated as already intended, and moderate parity changes became an accepted balance of payments weapon, instead of matters of political prestige? There is after all already a movement in this direction. The Managing Director of the I.M.F., M. Pierre-Paul Schweitzer, suggested in an important speech in Kingston, Ontario, on 2 June 1969 that there might be advantages in members proposing changes in parities whenever there was 'substantial evidence of fundamental disequilibrium and without necessarily waiting until such evidence was overwhelming'.

M. Schweitzer's speech did represent an encouraging step towards rationality in this area. But there are great difficulties in the way, quite apart from the British political fixation, mentioned above. The adjustable peg offers a one-way option to speculators: the direction of any change in the pound in 1967 or the D-mark in 1969 was after all obvious. The system is only workable because exchange rate changes are regarded as a measure of very last resort. Finance Ministers must deny that exchange rate changes are being contemplated; and these assurances will only carry credibility if Finance Ministers believe them themselves and are known to be fighting for existing parities. The penalty for failure, at least in the case of downward adjustments, has very often been their own departure.

Once such denials were completely dismissed as routine noise, torrents of funds would flow across the exchange at the slightest suggestion that a parity might be out of line. The present 'swap' system could not cope with such movements; as the Bundesbank's behaviour in the course of 1969 showed, creditor countries are unwilling to extend open-ended and unlimited credits – and understandably so.

What exactly is the harm that results from making lump-sum exchange rate adjustments, as late as possible, when everything else has been tried?

The best answer to this question would be a study of U.K. experience in the 1960s.[5] In general terms, however, if an imbalance is allowed to persist too long, a deficit country acquires an excessively home-based industrial and commercial structure, while the surplus country becomes excessively export-oriented. In the case of the deficit country this results partly from the inadequate level of exports (compared with that required to secure equilibrium) and partly from the back-door protection of home industry to which governments are driven. This makes adjustment needlessly painful and difficult when it does come, and there is a risk of high transitional unemployment while resources are being transferred. Shop assistants in Britain cannot be transferred overnight to engineering establishments which do not yet exist, while Volkswagen workers cannot move straight away into the German social services. These very facts themselves become ammunition for those who oppose parity changes, and the eventual adjustments are all the more sudden and severe, when at last they come.

In the case of a deficit country, which has debts to repay, a switch to surplus has to be crammed into a short period. This involves an extremely difficult attempt to cut or hold back home consumption. By contrast a more gradual and earlier method of adjustment would involve just small adjustments in its rate of increase.

Mr Roy Jenkins himself pointed out in his speech to the I.M.F. in September 1969 that one reason why governments have tended to resist parity changes 'has undoubtedly been' their effects 'on the stability of domestic monetary systems as well as the international effects of gains and losses to holders of currency balances'. A conventional-size devaluation involves a sudden inflationary shock, as import prices go up with a jump, and indirect taxes may also have to be raised as an anti-spending device. These increases tend to be projected into the future and aggravate inflationary expectations. This in turn means bigger wage settlements for a given pressure of demand for labour. It was unfortunate that Mr Jenkins did not draw the correct moral from his own remarks, but was side-tracked into a will-o'-the-wisp search for ways of punishing currency speculators.

Most of the shocks involved in fixed-rate adjustments would be avoided under a more flexible system. Table 2 shows the average annual depreciation of the pound sterling which would have occurred if the parity changes of the last few decades had been accomplished by equivalent annual adjustments.

Table 2

AVERAGE ANNUAL DEPRECIATION OF STERLING AGAINST THE DOLLAR

	% per annum
1913–68	1·28
1929–68	1·80
1939–68	1·77
1947–68	2·44

Source: *Hansard*, 21 January 1969.

Even under a flexible system, one could not hope for entirely even year-to-year movements. But we would have had a much better chance of avoiding the vicious cycle of debt, delay and demoralisation which characterised the 1960s. Under almost any conceivable form of flexible rate, the sterling rate would have begun to depreciate at least as early as 1960 when the first signs of chronic deficit emerged. British exports would gradually have become cheaper in overseas markets and also more profitable, relative to home production, while imports would have become more expensive. The opposite process would have been in motion for most of the decade for Germany, without the series of revaluation crises of 1960–1 and 1968–9. Financial policy in both countries would have been freer to concentrate on internal stability, with much less likelihood of a conflict between external and internal objectives.

5 The Wider Effects of 'Fixed Rates'

The purpose of this chapter is to explain some of the adverse effects of a 'fixed rate' regime that go well outside technical currency matters or subjects discussed in the financial columns. These justify a degree of feeling and indignation which might otherwise seem surprising in discussing topics of this kind.

It has been argued in the preceding pages that the balance of payments is a pseudo-problem arising from pegging exchange rates at an arbitrary level. If exchange rates were not pegged, or could be relied upon to be at the right level, there would be no specifically balance of payments problem, apart from the normal problem of keeping total spending of all kinds in line with resources. (Objections to this thesis will be considered in Part II.)

When exchange rates are fixed at an arbitrary level, £1 of foreign exchange may be worth more than £1 of home currency (or less for a surplus country). This means that prices and profits cannot perform their normal function, and saving foreign exchange becomes a national obsession. Issues are decided not on their own merits, but on whether they will discourage imports or give someone a hidden export advantage. These distortions are diminishing at the time of writing, because of the payments surplus. But they could occur again. Moreover, even if every major country were in balance, they would still not disappear, for all concerned would want to do their best to safeguard themselves against the fearsome prospect of future deficits. Thus while the obsession with saving and earning foreign exchange was particularly prominent in Britain in the 1960s, there were few countries from which it was entirely absent.

As many of the obvious ways of subsidising exports or keeping out imports are ruled out by international agreements or understandings, a great deal of balance of payments activity has consisted of a search for loopholes and side-effects, and the setting-up of innumerable semi-official organisations designed to persuade people to do things which it does not really pay them to do. Human beings work best when the pursuit of their own self-interest is reasonably conducive to the common good, or at least when divergences between private and social good are obvious from everyday experience (e.g. not emitting foul smoke from factories, or refraining from exploiting monopoly positions). Even government officials work better if given tangible objectives to pursue. Under a regime of fixed rates, however, citizens are expected to become amateur macro-economists in their daily lives. They are of course not equipped to do this, and supposed benefits to the 'balance of payments' are used as a pretext for every variety of interest group asking for special favours.

The attitude adopted towards Germany in its years of surplus was no more reasonable. Having very successfully turned their swords into ploughshares and avoided – for most of the 1960s – the inflation which is supposed to have contributed so much to the rise of Hitler, German citizens were given the impression that they were behaving badly. It was made to seem a crime that they were not consuming or inflating enough, and ordinary German citizens, who were hardly experts on the economics of exchange rates, were understandably resentful when the strength of their currency was made a cause of international reproach.

Opposition to flexible exchange rates is based on a questionable philosophy of governments. The level of home demand and exchange rates are two spheres where the Government has the power to make policy effective and influence events with reasonable speed. Yet the opponents of exchange rate flexibility reject action in the second of these spheres and think they can act instead (too often through exhortation) on the presumed deep-seated factors, such as managerial efficiency and industrial attitudes, where the Government has no direct power of responsibility and where any encouragement will take many years to produce an effect – and not necessarily have much relevance to the overseas balance when it does.

The following are a few specific examples of the irrational, and sometimes harmful, policies to which British Governments have been driven by the pseudo-problem of the balance of payments:

1. *The travel allowance*

This was the biggest interference with the personal freedom of adult citizens since the end of conscription. It was one of the largest onslaughts imaginable on what Sir Isaiah Berlin has called 'negative freedom'. For under the guise of hitting the rich, the allowance was a sweeping interference with the way in which individuals chose to spend their income.

It had the added offensiveness of bringing the law into contempt, and of being quite spurious in its egalitarianism. It did not affect those who wanted and could afford to travel to Sterling Area pleasure resorts in the West Indies. Nor did it affect those who could travel on private or official business, or who knew the ropes in other ways. In addition, those who could afford to maintain personal establishments overseas were inevitably hit less badly than those who could only afford to stay at hotels. The restriction put a premium on avoidance, stretching the rules and plain cheating.

The estimated savings (£25 million to £40 million per annum) were probably spurious. A large part of what appeared to be saved in the travel sector of the balance of payments was probably shifted to the 'balancing item'. Nevertheless, the rule could not be dismissed as entirely political. It was an effective *psychological demonstration of the need to save foreign exchange*, and was therefore supported by those who believed this to be a valid concept. When wages were frozen, credit squeezed and higher taxes imposed, there was an enormous temptation to go for something obvious, such as supposedly luxurious overseas spending, to buy public support for the rest of the package. Unfortunately, international organisations are much less strict in opposing restrictions on tourism than on direct trade.

At a later stage even the opponents of the restriction among politicians and officials, including Mr Roy Jenkins, were afraid to take them off 'too early' in case this should have led to demands for relaxation in other areas. The acceptance of the restriction for so long by the British public was either a sign of how low the lamp of liberty was really burning despite the so-called permissive society, or a reflection of widespread cynicism towards the law, or a mixture of both. If the possibility of travel restrictions being reimposed were the only consideration, this would be sufficient ground for being against 'fixed exchange rates'.

2. *Restrictions on overseas investment*

So long as an artificial exchange rate leads to a deficit or fear of a deficit, there is a standing temptation to gain foreign exchange at the expense of the future – even future foreign exchange earnings themselves – by restricting overseas investment. 'Left-wing' Labour M.P.s wanted to go further and secure and liquidate existing profit-earning assets, which might be labelled a policy of 'eating the seed corn'. The provision for 25 per cent surrender of the proceeds of private sales of overseas assets in the 'investment dollar' market was a small official step in this direction.

There may be some respectable arguments for a smaller amount of overseas investment than businessmen would undertake, if left to themselves. The advocates of restriction can, for example, talk about the leakage to foreign governments of tax payments on overseas profits – a leakage which does not occur on home investment, and which creates a discrepancy between the private and social rates of return. But the balance of payments obsession prevents governments from deciding policies on the merits of the issue and tempts them to scramble in times of difficulty for any foreign exchange saving they can find.

3. *Trade policy*

The way in which supposed balance of payments considerations aid and abet protectionism are pretty clear. Here are just a few examples:

(*a*) *Textiles from less-developed countries.* Foreign exchange pressures reinforce those from Lancashire against low-cost imports.

(*b*) *Government contracts.* With fixed exchange rates, and given British balance of payments history, Whitehall is reluctant to open official contracts, or those of the nationalised industries, to overseas tender. Under a flexible rate the whole issue would look very different.

(*c*) *Farm protection.* This again is decided neither on its social merits, nor on a realistic assessment of any gains in the terms of trade which might come about through being more self-sufficient in food, but on a crude foreign exchange saving basis. The only effective opposition comes from an equally crude Exchequer resistance to 'finding the money'. If the impending move from deficiency payments to levies takes place, this sort of resistance will be very much weakened. The U.K., which, owing to its small farm population, has had the good fortune to escape the agricultural crisis of the Continent, may bring these troubles upon itself, even outside the E.E.C., in an effort to 'save foreign exchange'.

(*d*) Similar foreign exchange arguments are used for 'supporting the aircraft industry', 'keeping the coalmines open', etc.

(*e*) Unilateral tariff cutting has been ruled out for balance of payments reasons, despite a comparatively severe British tariff with some very high peaks. The balance of payments provides a standing temptation to be cautious in international trade negotiations and to look for opportunities for smuggling in restrictions.

4. *Industrial policy*

Instead of encouraging the most efficient use of resources, industrial policy has been dominated by a search for back-door subsidies to exports and import barriers. A few examples make this obvious:

(*a*) State support has been provided for aluminium smelters.

(*b*) I.R.C. finance has been used to promote certain enterprises on favourable terms.

(*c*) An anti-service bias has influenced fiscal policy. This showed itself in the limitation of investment grants to manufacturing industry. It was again apparent in part of the original philosophy behind the Selective Employment Tax, and in the restriction of the Regional Employment Premium to manufacturing. All these devices were based on the calculation that the *average* export content of manufactured goods was higher than that of services, despite many individual exceptions. So long as the earning of foreign exchange was the supreme object of policy, and finer discrimination was ruled out by international undertakings, the case for these measures was much stronger than the then Opposition or the C.B.I. was prepared to admit.

(*d*) *Monopoly and merger policy*. Benefits to exports are one of the 'gateways' open to trade associations wishing to defend restrictive practices before the Court. (Such a defence has in fact rarely succeeded, but the position could always change.) The search for exports has also been one of the dominating motives in I.R.C.-inspired mergers. The balance of payments has been the most important single reason why the Government has avoided laying down definite rules in monopoly and industrial policy, and has preferred to rely on the judgment of politicians and officials rather than a known framework of law.

(*e*) More important than any single policy, an insidious scale of economic values is perpetuated. Companies should be judged, according to popular belief, not by the overall return on their assets, but by their export–import balance. Directors are all too ready to swallow this nonsense and indeed introduce their own exaggerations. Industries and firms begin to boast that they are more worthy of public esteem than their rivals because of their high export ratio, or the small net import content of their sales. Even the City of London has been known to use such bogus arguments. The mechanics of a fixed exchange rate hide the banal truth that the country could have a comparative advantage in processing goods with a very high import content indeed.

If a country were specially efficient in the polishing and painting of imported car bodies for re-export, or in entrepôt trade, these would be perfectly respectable activities and much more sensible than exporting bricks. Further reflection on these points casts doubt on the whole philosophy of the 'export drive' and certainly provides no excuse for the chauvinistic 'Buy British' drive which we have occasionally been threatened.

(*f*) Government departments, 'Little Neddies' and similar bodies, instead of doing their proper work, which is to look for areas where the price mechanism genuinely fails to work, are diverted into areas where the exchange rate and demand management could do the job much more efficiently. Thus far from being an argument for *laissez-faire*, a flexible exchange rate would allow government intervention to be more effective and less liable to be discredited, in those areas where it may have a worth-while function.

(*g*) It is worth mentioning, among the not-so-minor irritations, the way in which bank managers have to become unpaid government officials, deciding how 'essential' and export-promoting different categories of overdrafts really are.

None of the above arguments implies that the Government should abstain from all intervention in overseas trade. Central agencies for the provision of export advice of the kind provided by the Board of Trade or the British National Exports Council might still be justified even under a freely fluctuating exchange rate, because of economies of scale in such activities. There may or may not be special arguments for encouraging U.K. science-based industries. Some would argue that it may be possible to improve our terms of trade by increasing our self-sufficiency in, say, food and fuels (despite the substantial protection they already enjoy) instead of allowing free imports and paying for them by exports of manufactures. These questions have to be argued on their merits. A supporter of free trade would be well advised in today's world to support flexible rates. But the converse does not follow. A supporter of flexible rates is not logically committed to free trade. His argument is that a fixed exchange rate leads to a different – and in practice higher – degree and pattern of protection than would arise from a policy of maximising our advantages from international trade.

A very simple illustration should make this clear. Let us assume that at a time when the exchange rate is overvalued at $2.80 and the economy is not overheated, an overseas firm bids for a contract in a nationalised industry at a price of £10 million. If the order is accepted, demand has to be deflated enough to prevent the balance of payments deteriorating by £10 million. Because of the low profitability of additional exports in the assumed circumstances, the deflation of the home market does little to boost overseas sales, and most of the balance of payments saving must come on the import side. As imports are only a fifth of total expenditure, home spending must be cut down by up to £50 million – of which £40 million will represent a loss of home output and corresponding unemployment. The nearest home equivalent would therefore have to cost £50 million, before it paid to turn to imports. This point could be put across by discreetly asking the nationalised concern to conduct its policy on the assumption of a tariff of 400 per cent, or to employ a shadow exchange rate of $0.56 instead of the actual $2.80. This represent a far higher degree of protection than any conceivable 'optimum tariff' would provide if there were no payments problems.

Several considerations may dilute the starkness of this conclusion. One may argue about average and marginal propensities to import. Export profitability is a matter of degree, not of absolutes, and some extra goods may be sent overseas when the home market is deflated, even when the currency is overvalued. Moreover, with a lower pressure of home demand, costs and prices will rise less quickly, and over a number of years the overvaluation of the currency may be corrected.[6] Making all these allowances, any government interested in home output and employment would put extremely stiff deterrents on those foreign expenditures which it can by one means or another influence or control – far higher than the 0–30 per cent range of tariffs that might be under consideration if the balance of payments played no part.

After the exchange rate changes of the late 1960s and the very large balance of payments improvement in the winter of 1969–70, there were signs that the overriding concern with saving foreign exchange was diminishing. But long-acquired habits die hard, and it will be very tempting to keep alive a great deal of the apparatus and the mentality of 'saving foreign exchange' as an insurance against the pound becoming overvalued, an insurance that may be rational so long as we stick to 'fixed exchange rates'. These instincts will be reinforced by inflationary developments on the wages front and the possibility of E.E.C. entry. The most obvious sign in 1970 has been the campaign for increased agricultural protection, both as a preliminary to E.E.C. entry and for its own sake, which has been taken up so uncritically by the Conservative Party.

The logical position for the trade interventionist is to attempt to maximise Britain's real advantages on the assumption of payments balance, and leave the latter to be taken care of by a flexible exchange rate. Whether such intervention is worth-while at all is another question outside the scope of this book. At the time of writing, the various interventionist policies are something of a mixture. In some sectors they are based on terms of trade and other real income effects, on the assumption that overseas payments are in balance; but in other areas, the idea that exports are all-important and imports self-evidently undesirable is still rampant. Worst of all, the standard of public argument has been so debased that almost any special interest group seeking a tax relief subsidy or handout can secure a sympathetic hearing by invoking the magic of the balance of payments.

'Fixed exchange rates' have implications for many other aspects of government policy, far removed from any obvious concern with foreign trade. The following are a few of many examples:

1. *Payroll tax and social security contributions*

There may be a case for transferring some of the cost of the social services on to an employers' payroll levy of the kind familiar in some Continental countries. If the exchange rate is flexible, any resulting increase in labour costs can be compensated for in export markets by a downward adjustment in the price of a currency. If, on the other hand, the country is on a fixed rate, it would be better not to make the change, unless the Government is very sure that we are in chronic payments surplus. Otherwise even employers' pension contributions – let alone any more far-reaching move to a payroll tax – count as an addition to labour costs and so a potential threat to the balance of payments. Indeed, in situations of payments deficit there may be a case for refunding some of the existing employers' contributions via the Exchequer, to reduce direct labour costs as a back-door devaluation device.

2. *Equal pay for women*

This too can hit the balance of payments by raising labour costs in export industries. Under a fixed rate it would be highly logical to give great weight to this aspect, but not under a flexible system.

3. *The possibility of a shift from direct to indirect taxation, perhaps with the aid of a value-added tax*

It is absurd that such a long-term structural question should be decided by whether it adds or subtracts one or two percentage points from the devaluation advantages gained in 1967. But under a fixed rate this may be the most relevant aspect of all.

4. *Incomes policy*

This is not the place to discuss the substantive argument. The point here is that such policies have been taken at times beyond the point that would otherwise be desirable for the sake of (real or imaginary) balance of payments benefits. Distortions such as dividend or price control, and an anti-profit and anti-dividend bias, have been introduced into policy in an (unsuccessful) attempt to sell restraint to the unions. Incidentally, a policy of productivity bargaining, which is not foolproof and stimulates money earnings even more than it does productivity, could, under a flexible rate, still be worth while because it increases real wealth. But under a fixed rate such bargains may on balance be harmful because of their balance of payments effects. Under a fixed rate, incomes policy has to focus almost entirely on *money* wages and prices rather than on real effects on efficiency and incentives. Indeed it is an examination of the many structural changes which are ruled out, delayed or watered down for balance of payments reasons that provides some of the strongest arguments for flexibility.

There are even broader implications going way outside what is normally regarded as economic policy at all. Here again are a few examples:

1. *Arms sales to Nigeria, South Africa, Middle East, etc.*

Arms orders are always commercially tempting whether the exchange rate is fixed or floating. But when the exchange rate is fixed – and there is a risk of future pressure on it – the temptation to accept arms orders, whatever the political consequences, becomes overwhelming; a rational weighing of the commercial gain against the possible political damage becomes almost impossible.

2. *Overseas defence spending*

Again it is absurd that the decision about Britain's overseas commitments should be taken not on the basis of the total resource costs involved, or on a general judgment of Britain's role in the world, but as a by-product of balance of payments arithmetic.

3. *Dependence on U.S. in times of sterling crisis*

An even more serious matter has been the political effect of British dependence on the Americans to support the pound in times of crisis. It was often alleged that the British support initially given to the U.S. in Vietnam was connected with American help for sterling in critical phases. There is no need to assess the exact degree of truth in this allegation. These matters are usually referred to in such vague and tacit terms, even by those most directly involved, that concepts of truth or falsity are difficult to apply. The relevant point is the effect of large short-term international indebtedness arising from an overvalued currency on a country's foreign policy. Whether valid or not, suspicions will always occur when a country is maintaining an overvalued foreign exchange rate with the aid of its political allies.

4. *Aid to underdeveloped countries*

It is absurd to suppose that either the U.S. or Britain cannot 'afford' aid for poorer countries. There may be arguments against the effectiveness or desirability of aid, but the balance of payments argument is an entirely spurious one derived from the arbitrary fixing of exchange rates. It is on a par with the regulations requiring PX stores serving U.S. forces overseas to import their beer from the United States to save foreign exchange expenditure. American embassies in Europe at one time even had to buy U.S. wine for this reason.

There is one common feature to the examples of the effects of fixed exchange rates given in this chapter. They all lead to irrational criteria being applied in foreign or domestic policy. Many of them, too, are harmful to a free economy and even a free society. Nothing has done more to undermine the case for liberal economic policies, especially in the trade sphere, than 'fixed exchange rates' and the interventions they seemed to justify. Nothing, too, has done more to undermine the idea of a government of rules rather than of men in domestic policy, and to lend bogus patriotic support for those who believe that vast discretionary powers should be given to government organisations or – even worse – that the 'requests' of those in authority should be treated by the citizens as if they had the force of law.

The difficulty about treating an obsession is that those who see it for what it is and wish to remove it have to become obsessional themselves. Until recently the exchange rate was the one untouchable in British politics. The British devaluation and the Continental exchange rate changes, together with discussions of the subject by the I.M.F., have lessened the taboo a little, but have by no means removed it. The idea of allowing the exchange rate to move by the amount required as a normal event is still regarded as dangerous and unsound. If any other element in British life – whether the standard rate of income tax, or some quirk in the legal system – were to be treated in this way, it would also enter into every other problem, and those who wanted to remove its privileged status would seem obsessional. All the economic commentator can do is to point to the self-created nature of the economic sickness from which Britain was supposed to have suffered in the 1960s, and to the irrationalities, distortions, material losses and sacrifices of personal liberty involved in regarding exchange rates as ends rather than means.

PART TWO

The Case for Flexibility

Part I of this book discussed the widespread damage inflicted by the attempt to maintain 'fixed exchange rates'; and the various forms of flexibility were briefly listed. The present Part is concerned with the more constructive task of examining the case for flexibility in the light of the objections most frequently raised against it. It is therefore almost entirely in 'question and answer' form. The largest amount of space is devoted to floating rates, which are covered in Chapter 7. As this is the most thoroughgoing reform, a discussion of it brings out many of the underlying issues. The heart of the argument is in that chapter, where it is shown how different present arrangements are from a system of genuinely fixed rates in which traders and governments could put their trust. Chapter 8 deals with compromise proposals for gradually moving parities which are currently on the international agenda. It also discusses some of the balance of payments issues raised by Britain's application for E.E.C. membership. As exchange rate flexibility would provide more freedom of action in domestic demand management, it seems only fair to give readers a personal summary of the state of the debate on this subject, which is provided in the Appendix. This will show that advocacy of flexibility need have no connection with being 'soft on inflation'.

Before discussing ways of changing exchange rates, it is, however, necessary to deal with any doubts about their role in balance of payments adjustment. It has already been argued that payments surpluses and deficits do – subject to what has been said about demand management – simply reflect the pattern of exchange rates, and can usually be put right without more 'fundamental treatment'. The following chapter deals with the doubts that have sometimes been expressed on this matter.

6 Are Exchange Rates Important?

Surely, even before the 1967 devaluation, British prices and costs were no higher than those abroad? Prices matter less nowadays than design, delivery dates, salesmanship and service.

The single most important – and widely ignored – sentence in the Brookings Report on the U.K. reads: 'There is no logical connection between the causes of a country's payments deficit and the appropriate solution.'[7] A country may fail to pay its way even if its prices are low by international standards. This may reflect bad salesmanship, original sin or the offsetting of a commercial surplus by military spending overseas. Whatever the reason, if overseas commitments are maintained, export prices have to be reduced still further or export profit margins increased, and imports need to be made more expensive or less profitable.

The effects of exchange rate changes on the comparative profitability of exports, imports and production for the home market are very important. After a devaluation it may pay exporters to keep up their prices in overseas currencies, but increase their profit margins, and the main stimulus to exports may even come in this direction. Similarly importers may not increase their prices, but accept for the time being lower or even negative profit margins. Revaluations, of course, work in the opposite direction, making exports less profitable and imports more so. Indeed, if international markets were all 'perfect' and deatl in standardised articles with no goodwill attached – as is the case for some metals, grains or shares – only one price would be possible for any commodity. Exchange rate changes and changes in international cost levels would both work entirely through their effects on the relative profitability of production for home and overseas markets.

Owing to the operation of goodwill, sales promotion, traditional connections, product differentiation and similar forces, the prices of many internationally traded goods supplied by different countries can differ from each other. Thus a tendency to overvaluation will often show itself in price movements for which data, although imperfect, are easier to obtain than for profitability. British export prices, for example, rose faster than those of competitor countries in the years up to 1967. The N.I.E.S.R. indices show that prices of British exports of manufactures had risen by 20 per cent between 1958 and the third (pre-devaluation) quarter of 1967 compared with 9 per cent for a weighted average of other industrial countries. In the two years following devaluation the ground lost since 1960–1 was recovered.

There are, however, no figures comparing the absolute level of export prices for different countries at different times, and it would be very difficult to make a meaningful computation. There are very good reasons for expecting the exchange rate required to balance a country's overseas payments (the 'equilibrium exchange rate') to diverge considerably from that suggested by the internal purchasing power of its currency (its 'purchasing power parity'). This arises from the existence of products which do not enter into international trade. These tend to be predominantly, but by no means exclusively, 'services'. Prices of a country's traded goods will have to be roughly comparable to those of its trading partners. On the other hand non-traded services can vary enormously from country to country, as is confirmed by all the travellers' tales about the varying cost of a haircut or a restaurant meal in different parts of the world. There is a good deal of evidence that the richer countries have a much greater productivity advantage in goods than in non-traded services. In addition, countries enjoying more rapidly growing overall productivity than average tend to show larger differential gains in the goods than in the services sector.

The relative price level of services in relation to traded goods will therefore tend to be higher in the richer countries, and this means that the overall price level or 'cost of living' will also be higher there. Service prices will also increase more rapidly in relation to goods in the more rapidly growing countries. Their overall price levels will therefore also increase faster, even if equilibrium rates of exchange prevail. This is in fact what we find. The cost of living is higher in the U.S.A. than in Britain and lower in many of the 'developing countries', and it has risen more quickly in the last decade in Germany and Japan than in the U.K. (if allowance is made for exchange rate changes).[8] Such considerations cannot determine the exact equilibrium exchange rate of a currency, but they do help to explain what would otherwise seem puzzling discrepancies.

But is not international trade taking more and more the form of highly sophisticated capital goods, for which price is less and less important?

Even if this were correct, the point about profitability would still apply. But the basic assertions in the question amount to little more than fashionable gossip for which evidence is rarely produced. In the first place there is nothing to suggest that sophisticated capital goods are becoming preponderant in international trade. One could equally assert that international trade is more likely to grow in mass tourism or consumer goods which are highly price-sensitive. The following breakdown of the growth of British visible trade in manufactures is interesting:

Table 3
U.K. TRADE IN FINISHED MANUFACTURES

	*Capital goods**	*Consumer goods*
Exports in 1967	£1,990 m.	£531 m.
Rate of increase per annum, 1957–67	5·3%	5·5%
Imports in 1967	£905 m.	£339 m.
Rate of increase per annum, 1957–67	16·7%	16·4%

* S.I.T.C. Revised, Sections 7 and 8.
Source: Board of Trade.

The dividing line between 'highly sophisticated' capital goods and the rest comes somewhere inside the capital goods section and is difficult to identify from the statistical categories. But the above figures do at least show that there has been no significant tendency for consumer goods to lose out to capital goods on either the export or import side.

It is also far from self-evident that the final demand for particular types of computer, or supersonic aircraft (or econometricians) is insensitive to price. The belief that it is may be a short-run illusion, based on the fact that the development of substitutes takes time. Nor should it be forgotten that all these articles are made up of many simpler components and processed materials, and the mix of ingredients will be highly sensitive to the prices offered by rival suppliers. One is tempted to ask why, if the demand for sophisticated capital goods is so insensitive, exporters of them do not increase their charges indefinitely and thus boost profits.

How about the 'kinked demand curve'? In other words, if you raise your export price you do so alone, but if you lower it, your competitors will follow you down.

There is a limit to the extent they can afford to do so if you devalue sufficiently and if they do not. If their governments threaten to devalue too to prevent this, it is an admission that exchange rate changes are effective weapons, and the real problem is one of incompatible balance of payments aims by different countries.

More fundamentally, the kinked demand curve is a short-term phenomenon. It does not explain why the kink is where it is. By one means or another the kink will eventually shift its position to a level at which market demand is met at a normal commercial profit by the typical supplier. The effect of a devaluation – or of a sufficient slowdown in the rate of inflation – in a supplying country is to lower this maintainable long-run price and displace those marginal producers who cannot afford to meet it.

Is there nevertheless any evidence of price sensitivity in international trade?

The presumption that international price elasticities are likely to be substantial follows from the fact that a country's exports of any manufactured article are likely to be a small proportion of the world total;

Table 4
RELATIONSHIP BETWEEN RELATIVE PRICE MOVEMENTS AND TRADE SHARES

	% change in export price index of manufactures, 1958–67	*Share of total, 1957* %	*Share, 1967* %	*Change, 1957–67* %
Japan	−7	6·0	9·8	+3·8
Italy	−6	4·1	7·0	+2·9
France	+6	8·6	8·5	−0·1
West Germany	+14	18·5	+19·7	+1·2
U.S.A.	+15	23·3	20·5	−3·2
U.K.*	+20	18·1	11·9	−7·2

* Up to third quarter of 1967.
Source: N.I.E.S.R.

and it would not take a vast reduction in price to secure a pretty large increase in sales.

The above crude comparison of export prices and trade shares is not in itself conclusive, as many other factors apart from relative price changes were responsible for the experiences recorded. German exports clearly enjoyed certain non-price advantages. Nevertheless, the relationship over a period of years between relative price movements and trade shares, shown in Table 4, is too striking to be the product of pure coincidence. This is particularly so for the U.K.

The relationship shown in the table would be less clear-cut, although still in the same direction, if some of the smaller countries were included. This is not surprising, as smaller countries have less diversified export structures heavily influenced by market trends for particular commodities.

The period after 1967 has been excluded from the above table, to show the U.K.'s pre-devaluation experience. In the subsequent two years export prices measured in dollars fell by 4–5 per cent, while the weighted average for all industrial countries rose by 4 per cent. Not surprisingly, the U.K. share of world trade, which is measured in

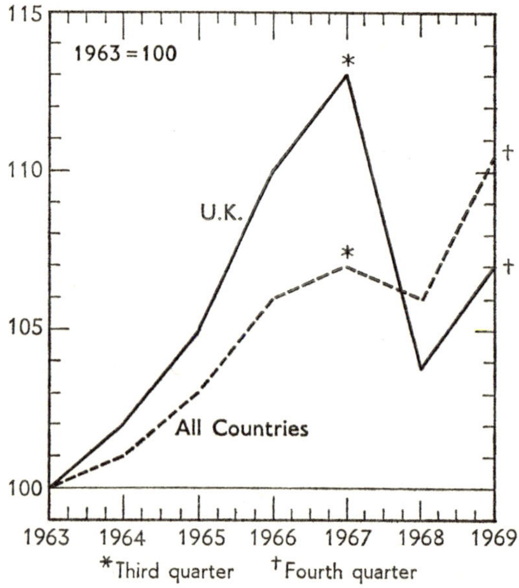

FIG. 1

Prices of Exports of Manufactures.
Source: National Institute and Board of Trade.

dollars, fell again on the N.I.E.S.R. figures to 11·1 per cent in 1968. But from the second quarter of 1968 until at least the early part of 1970 it stayed almost constant at that level.

Statistical calculations of international trade elasticities are full of snags and pitfalls, and no set of calculations based on the average experience of several countries can be regarded as reliable for any particular surplus or deficit country. This is one reason for preferring flexible rates to occasional parity changes which require a Government to make a guess about elasticities which it will be unable to revise for many years to come. Generally speaking, the early post-war calculations, which were subsequently severely criticised, gave low price elasticities, while more recent calculations give higher values. The Brookings Institution used an I.M.F. estimate of approximately 2 for the elasticity of demand for British exports of manufactures, implying that a 1 per cent reduction in export prices relative to that of competitors leads to a 2 per cent increase in volume. Brookings also assumed an elasticity of import demand for finished manufactures of 2·7 and of 1·1 for semi-manufactured goods.[9] (Maurice FG. Scott, in a study published in the early 1960s, estimated an elasticity of as much as 7 for imports of finished manufactures.)[10] The 1970 White Paper on the economic effects of E.E.C. membership assumed a range of $1\frac{1}{2}$–$2\frac{1}{2}$ for the elasticity of demand for exports and of $\frac{1}{3}$–$1\frac{1}{2}$ per cent for non-food imports. All these values are amply sufficient to secure international balance in response to moderate exchange rate changes, even before bringing in the profitability effect.

The above discussion implies that devaluation will turn the terms of trade against the devaluing country; is it not better to avoid this?

A devaluation will often, although not invariably, worsen the terms of trade. But so in such circumstances will any other method of adjustment, with the arguable exception of a retreat towards protection. The change in the terms of trade is moreover usually much less than the nominal amount of the devaluation. The 1967 U.K. devaluation was officially 14·3 per cent (in practice less because of the withdrawal of the export rebate). The resulting deterioration in the terms of trade in 1968–9 was about 3 per cent. This was the equivalent to a loss of £200 million to £300 million of the annual G.N.P. of that period, or little more than $\frac{1}{2}$ per cent.[11] The total shift of resources to exports and import saving in 1968–9 was by contrast about £1,000 million, equivalent to some $2\frac{1}{2}$ per cent of the G.N.P. Thus much the greater part of the resources shift was due simply to the need to move from deficit to surplus. A great many of the arguments against exchange rate changes at times of deficit are really arguments against eliminating the deficit at all.

A deficit may just reflect the fact that prices of a country's internationally traded goods and services have risen too fast for payments equilibrium. This means that it has been acquiring its imports on the cheap, and its terms of trade have become artificially favourable by the eve of devaluation. The exchange rate change thus is just a belated adjustment to internal inflation, and the terms of trade go back to where they would have been if the country's costs and prices had stayed in the right relation to the rest of the world's from the beginning.

A deficit may on the other hand, as already mentioned, reflect a deterioration in competitive power unconnected with price; or it may reflect an increase in non-commercial spending overseas. In that case the deterioration in the terms of trade represents, not a restoration of a former *status quo*, but a price concession to persuade foreign buyers to purchase more from the country concerned. In such a case a real deterioration in the terms of trade is unavoidable, whether it is accomplished by devaluation or accomplished by unaided deflation. (The U.K. deficit in the 1960s was a combined result of price inflation and deterioration in non-price aspects.)

A much more interesting point is that two kinds of terms of trade change are involved in an exchange rate change. There is the change in the terms of trade with the outside world, just discussed. Where, however, a U.K. exporter takes the benefit of devaluation in his profit margin, he increases his sterling prices in a way that is not open to a purely home-market producer. There is thus a shift in the domestic 'terms of trade' in favour of the exporter (or the producer of import substitutes) against the purely home-market producer. This may be the most important effect of all, but is rarely discussed at all explicitly.

May not a country's deficit (or surplus) be so deep-rooted that no feasible exchange rate would eliminate it?

This objection cannot logically be advanced by those who believe that incomes policy or a higher margin of unemployment to hold down costs and prices would help to prevent payments deficits. For all such policies, if they work at all, work in exactly the same way as exchange rate changes, i.e. by acting on export and import prices and profit margins. They would make no sense if neither price nor profitability changes could bring about adjustment. Even a great many of the more interventionist industrial policies, such as the provision of cheap finance for aluminium smelters, are designed to increase the profitability of exports or import substitutes and thus work in the same way as a (very small) exchange rate change.

There has been considerable academic argument about whether there could be a freak case in which no change in a country's cost and prices or in its exchange rate, however drastic, could bring about equilibrium in a country's balance of payments. (Readers uninterested in academic considerations might prefer to skip to the top of p. 44.) It is frequently stated that for a change in relative prices, whether brought about by devaluation or internal policy, to succeed in improving the current balance, the sum of elasticities of export and import demand must exceed 1. Even if this were correct, the condition is not particularly severe. We have already seen that in most empirical international trade studies, including those concerned with U.K. devaluation, the export elasticity alone is taken as at least $1\frac{1}{2}$ and possibly a good deal higher. The formula is, moreover, a deliberate oversimplification, which overstates the difficulties of adjustment. For it applies only when supply is perfectly elastic on both sides of the frontier – which involves, *inter alia*, exporters taking out the whole of their devaluation advantage in overseas price reductions. In other conditions even lower demand elasticities will do the trick. If the elasticities are perverse, it means that a small change in the exchange rate will make the current balance of payments worse.

Even then, an equilibrium could still come about in two ways. When elasticities are perverse, an exchange rate *appreciation* will reduce a deficit and might bring about equilibrium – although there are various reasons why this is unlikely in practice. A more probable alternative is that as the exchange rate is lowered and imports become more and more expensive while exports sell at ever more favourable bargain prices in overseas markets, demand elasticities will increase until they are sufficient to close the deficit. The theoretical question does not turn on the elasticities in the vicinity of the prevailing exchange rate, but on whether there is any price at all, however depressed, at which the demand for a country's currency will equal the supply.

This controversy is analysed in the works cited in the references. Fortunately there is no need to discuss it here. For the opponents of relying entirely on changes in exchange rates do not have to prove that *no* exchange rate will provide an equilibrium. All they have to show is that international elasticities are sufficiently adverse (not necessarily perverse) that an extremely large unfavourable shift in the terms of trade would be required to bring about a small improvement in the balance of payments. In that case the pursuit of equilibrium by a country highly dependent on international trade may lead to impoverishment. Imagine for example a country with a sole exportable commodity, say coffee, of which it has a world monopoly. Let us call it 'Brazil', remembering that this is a caricature which bears little relation to the modern country of that name. Situations may arise in which unrestricted free trade at the equilibrium exchange rate would lead to a very low world price for coffee and very adverse terms of trade for 'Brazil'.

It is important to note that 'Brazil's' plight in this example does not depend in the least on the use of the exchange rate as a balance of payments regulator. It would be just as great in a gold standard world in which 'Brazilian' costs and prices fell sufficiently to avoid a gold drain, or in a world of barter in which coffee was directly exchanged for imported commodities. 'Brazil's' problem is a real and not a monetary one. It arises from the country's heavy dependence on a commodity for which world demand is near saturation point. The possibility of alleviation arises from 'Brazil's' monopoly position, which allows it to raise the coffee price by withholding supplies. If a country threatened with poverty has such monopoly powers, it should use them regardless of the balance of payments. This could be achieved by putting a uniform surcharge on all imports or on all exports. This would lead to a balance at a lower level of trade, and therefore a smaller volume of coffee sales, which would improve 'Brazil's' terms of trade.

Never mind 'Brazil'. Do you think that the U.K. today does actually suffer from adverse elasticities? After all, devaluation took a long time to work.

Adverse elasticities are extremely unlikely for an industrial country with a diversified economy. There has not been a single case in recent years of a moderate devaluation, which once it has been *backed up by effective internal financial policies* has failed to restore international balance in an advanced industrial country. This applies to France after 1958, Canada after 1962 and the U.K. after 1967. Even the 5 per cent German revaluation of 1961 did help for a time to remove the German surplus. (It is too early at the time of writing to pronounce on the French move of 1969, although the omens seem good.)

Exchange rate changes do perhaps take longer to affect the current balance of payments in Britain than in some other countries. If this is so, it is probably because the British export problem has been partly a capacity one, in the long-term sense that production facilities, design and sales organisation have not in the past been of a kind that could be easily or quickly switched to the export market, whatever exchange rate or home-demand policies were followed. The composition of productive capacity has been excessively biased towards home-market requirements. The U.K.'s long-term problem is to secure more investment, in human as well as physical resources, designed to cater for world, rather than British, markets. The reason for the reluctance of British businessmen to adjust their plans immediately after the 1967 devaluation was an extreme suspicion that any profitability or price advantage in overseas markets would soon be eroded, and that export markets were an 'unreliable' basis for expansion. There has after all been a historical tendency for such erosion to take place after each devaluation, but the process takes more years than is generally imagined.

Businessmen are proverbially excessively sceptical of the effectiveness of price competition. Yet even those who were most sceptical of the 1967 devaluation argued that something larger would indeed have boosted sales. (Many of the firms taking part in a study by the Manchester Centre for Business Research expressed disappointment at the smallness of the devaluation.)[12] They may have been wrong about the size of the exchange rate needed in 1967, but their response hardly suggests that their overseas business is impervious to price or profitability considerations. The very fact that other governments might not have allowed us to get away with a larger fixed rate devaluation suggests that they too believed that exchange rate changes had a large effect on international sales and competitive power.

What would you propose if, despite what you have just said, the U.K. could only achieve a balance, in some future period of difficulty, at an exchange rate which involved intolerably unfavourable terms of trade?

In such a situation the Government might be justified in exploiting any monopoly power the country had, either as a buyer or a seller, to improve the country's equilibrium terms of trade. A surcharge on all overseas payments – which could cover invisibles, travel and capital outflows as well as visible imports – combined with a flexible exchange rate, would give nearly all the help possible in the circumstances.

The size of the deficit at an arbitrary exchange rate is a misleading guide to what could or should be done. The crucial point is that (as we saw in the case of 'Brazil') anything that can be prudently done to improve the terms of trade can be accomplished by commercial policy, while allowing a flexible exchange rate to look after the balance of payments. It would be highly irrational to add to the nation's difficulties in such circumstances by deflating output and employment and wasting our resources to maintain an arbitrary parity. Nor would one need the paraphernalia of physical import restrictions or back-door industrial intervention.

Should such a surcharge, imposed to improve the terms of trade, be uniform for all payments and on all commodities?

In principle, a government could impose different surcharges on different imports (and exports), and on different trading partners, to make the most of this country's monopoly buying and selling power, which varies from sector to sector. Such a Schachtian policy would not only be a display of bad neighbourliness, but the Government would – partly through ignorance and partly because of political pressure by producers – almost certainly get the pattern of charges badly wrong.

It scarcely needs to be added that the assumptions behind the last two questions do not represent a reasonable view of Britain's situation. There is much more to be said for the view expressed in a document published by the Confederation of British Industries in 1970, entitled *Britain in the World*, in the following words:

> To make efficient use of our resources we need to work – with due reciprocity from those nations who can afford it – towards freer international trade and investment, yet balance of payments pressures force us to place obstacles in the way of both. There is always the plea of necessity, but its degree and the urgency of its demands are matters for judgment. In making this judgment we believe that Britain should continue to give priority to a liberal commercial policy and exert the degree of responsibility and bargaining power that fall to her as the world's third largest trader, both to avoid provoking any retreat from free trade by others as a result of her own actions and to see they meet their international obligations in full measure.[13]

To pursue this theme would, however, be a digression from the main purpose of this book. The relevant point here is the need to separate commercial from balance of payments policy. The surplus or deficit that exists at an arbitrary exchange rate is quite irrelevant to the decision (which may be made for us by the E.E.C.) about where to pitch our policy between unilateral free trade and extreme Schachtianism. Once this choice has been made, we can leave it to exchange rate movements and demand management to balance our overseas payments. Nothing but confusion arises from mixing the two sets of issues.

7 Objections to Floating Rates

Many discussions of the subject fail to distinguish between:

(*a*) the relative merits of fixed and floating rates once in operation, and

(*b*) the problem of transition from fixed to floating rates, and the choice of time to float.

The problems of transition are discussed on p. 64, in connection with the inflationary issue. For the moment we are concerned with the first set of problems.

How can the businessman hope to cope with the uncertainty if he does not know what he will receive for his exports, or what his raw materials will cost?

In more or less sophisticated form, this is far and away the most common objection to floating rates. One might remark *en passant* that fear of uncertainty and unstable prices has been one of the standard defences of every restrictive practice, cartel or price ring in all walks of business.

If one considers it seriously, this fear is based on four fallacies:

(1) It assumes that serious exchange risk is absent from the present system.

(2) It overlooks the possibilities of transferring the exchange risk to professional operators by means of the forward market and other devices.

(3) It ignores the risks, uncertainties and increased government interference with business arising from the attempt to maintain wrongly valued parities.

(4) It assumes that floating rates need be wildly fluctuating rates.

(1) On this point the C.B.I. study *Britain in the World*, already quoted in the previous chapter, remarks that 'the stability of the present system is somewhat illusory because of the possibility of sudden changes in parities'. After the changes in the sterling, mark and franc parities (together with those of many smaller countries) in 1967–9 and the uncertainties subsequently hanging over a number of other countries'

currencies, businessmen should need little reminding of this point. The moderate probability of a 10–20 per cent devaluation (or a somewhat smaller revaluation), which has dogged several currencies over the last few years, is at least as great a business uncertainty as the high probability of a change of a few percentage points each year under a floating system. Many large companies which place contracts several years ahead would not dream at present of leaving themselves exposed to currency risks. Smaller companies who do not know, or are not able to take advantage of, such protective arrangements can be caught out badly under the present system.

(2) The best-known method of protection against exchange risk is, of course, the forward market, in which the ordinary trader can buy or sell his foreign exchange ahead of requirements. In the winter of 1969–70, the average premium on the dollar for delivery in three months' time averaged around $\frac{1}{8}$ per cent (or $\frac{1}{2}$ per cent at an annual rate). If the importer has to bear an additional burden when there is a premium on the dollar, the exporter who sells his dollars forward receives a bonus. The net cost of forward facilities to all who use them is the dealers' spread between buying and selling rates.

The forward premium on the dollar – or discount on sterling – has of course at times been much higher when sterling has been distrusted. At times in 1969 it touched 9 per cent, measured at an annual rate. These sudden jumps to very high levels are of course a great nuisance to business, but they are a symptom of fixed rates under suspicion. If the 'spot' rate is free to move, as it is under a floating system (or if the official parity is trusted), spot and forward rates will not diverge too far from each other. For if they did, it would pay operators to buy spot and sell forward or vice versa. (The spot–farward gap would then reflect approximately the interest differentials between the currency centres concerned, except to the extent that exchange controls brought about discrepancies.)

Forward exchange facilities, like other types of business service, tend to respond to demand. A few years ago the normal contract was three months, and six months or a year were a rarity. Now yearly contracts are quite common and rates for two, three or more years ahead can be quoted on request. Further developments could certainly be expected under a more flexible system.

It would be foolish to pretend that there are no difficulties, or that all would be plain sailing if only the pound floated. For periods of over a year ahead markets tend to be thin, and even for shorter periods the very largest international companies are afraid to deal too heavily for fear of their own commercial weight. There are, moreover, certain countries where governments do all they can to discourage forward transactions in their currencies.

Forward contracts are far from being the only way of coping with currency uncertainties. An equivalent technique is to borrow in the country where receipts are due or (if exchange control allows) to deposit funds in the country where there are commitments for future payments. Another method of coping with long-term contracts is to invoice either in sterling or in a currency such as dollars or D-marks. Dollar invoicing is now normal practice for some of the large oil companies outside the Sterling Area. Moreover, some long-term contracts already have a renegotiation clause for raw material or other cost changes of a kind which would automatically cover exchange rate changes in supplying countries.

It is often forgotten that there are very considerable risks in quoting firm prices for long-term contracts even if no exchange risk is foreseen. Wages rates and raw material prices cannot be accurately predicted. Nor can taxes, credit squeezes or government policy in either the seller or the customer country. A floating rate might well reduce the total risk. An automatic currency depreciation under a flexible rate would provide an exporter under long-term contract with built-in compensation for an unexpected acceleration in the rate of inflation in his home country. He would not receive this under a 'fixed rate' which his government had managed to hold for the length of the contract.

(3) The various methods of dealing with longer-term exchange risk are not foolproof or free from political interference, and they are certainly a nuisance. Of course it would be more convenient if exchange rates never changed and overseas transactions were just like domestic ones, except for the use of different units. Such exchange rate rigidity would itself imply more stability than exists at present in relative international costs and prices. Unfortunately this comparison is based on a dream world far removed from the reality of the present 'fixed rate system'. The latter amounts, in the words of the C.B.I. study, to a 'reversal of ends and means'. As it explains:

> To resist changes in parities, deficit countries have, of necessity, introduced restrictions on imports, exports and capital movements. These restrictions, which can be of a fiscal, exchange control or other administrative nature, represent some of the costs of maintain-

ing the present system, since all restrictions on trade and capital movements impede the exercise of sound business judgment in the management and development of industry, thereby reducing the efficiency of the economy.

One might add that the effort to preserve exchange rates leads to all kinds of sudden and unpredictable government subsidies to overseas competitors on balance of payments pretexts, stop–go measures and the abrupt imposition of domestic credit squeezes. The latter are often accompanied by economically damaging price-freezes or dividend controls. Despite all these interferences, exchange rates are liable to move by large jumps, so that the bother of exchange protection cannot be avoided after all. It is questionable whether such an environment is more stable and conducive to trade than one where the exchange rate gradually adjusts itself to changing market forces, and fully developed forward markets are available.

A floating rate would also reduce, although probably not eliminate, the temptation of governments to embark on the currency controls or interference with forward markets which can make exchange cover difficult under the present system. As the C.B.I. Council has stressed:

> The chief advantage of a floating rate system is that it would enable international trade and investment to be substantially freed from the controls associated with the maintenance of fixed rates of exchange, although there would undoubtedly be some time-lag between the introduction of floating rates and the removal of the controls.[14]

In addition governments could, under a floating rate, give credible assurances to industry that export profitability could be maintained and that demand would be allowed to grow in line with productive capacity. The removal of present misgivings and uncertainty on these subjects is surely worth something to business as well as to the wider community.

(4) The belief that floating rates are likely to be wildly fluctuating rates lies at the heart of much of the opposition to them. As Professor Milton Friedman has pointed out, being in favour of floating rates does not mean being in favour of unstable rates. The aim is a system in which exchange rates are free to flucutate, but in fact move within moderate ranges 'because basic economic policies and conditions are stable'.[15]

It is a common mistake to equate a free market with a violently unstable one. A distinction must be made between a steep *fall* in a rate and wild fluctuations around a trend. If there are steep falls under a floating rate, they will be due to internal disturbances, which would cause severe difficulties with a fixed rate, and eventually bring a devaluation. Sharp *fluctuations* would on the other hand be unlikely. Market operators will gain by buying when the rate is low and selling when it is high, thus smoothing out market movements. Speculators will make profits for themselves by reducing the amplitude of fluctuations around the trend and make losses if they act in a destabilising way, and professional speculators who make losses will not stay long in business. Under a floating rate, there would be a much greater incentive to study the true background, for example, to the British trade figures. This would contrast with the agonising period from November 1967 to the summer of 1969, when the possible losses of speculators who took a too gloomy view on a single month's figures were modest, but when the gains from a second devaluation, or a sudden withdrawal of the exchange rate peg, would have been considerable.

Are there not wide fluctuations in the stock and commodity markets, whether despite or because of the presence of speculators?

Speculative activity can be destabilising under special circumstances. A large amount of speculation may be undertaken by a shifting population of amateurs, and by ordinary traders as ancillary activities to their main business. Speculators as a group could then make losses for considerable periods. If in addition speculative activity comes to predominate over normal trading, it may then pay even the minority of professional speculators to predict what the rest of the market is going to think, rather than worry about fundamental forces. The motto then is to join every bull and bear market, but get out in time.

An unstable market of this kind cannot be ruled out *a priori*. But there are reasons for expecting a free foreign exchange market to be fairly stable in practice. Because of the rough relation between equilibrium exchange rates and movements of national price levels, there is a band of exchange rates which can be regarded as 'normal', and this will prevent speculative waves from getting out of hand (see p. 37). This is where the foreign exchange market differs from both stock and commodity markets, where the concept of a normal price is much more elusive. The currency of an advanced industrial country can be used to purchase a vast number of goods, services and capital assets most of which are close substitutes of other goods, services and assets. A fall in the price of a currency is therefore likely to attract a large amount of non-speculative supporting purchases. In this a currency differs from a commodity like tin or wheat, which has a narrow range of uses and for which demand is likely to be inelastic.

You have discussed trade and short-term financial movements at considerable length. But what would be the effect of long-term capital movements on a floating rate?

If an exchange rate depreciates, the cost of an overseas asset increases; but so does the return measured in the home currency. So there is little net change in the attractiveness of the transaction. If, however, the home currency has fallen to a level from which it is expected to recover, it pays an intending overseas investor to buy the asset now rather than wait. Conversely, if there is a temporary appreciation in the home currency, it pays the investor to wait in the hope of buying it more cheaply. There is, of course, a limit to the extent to which companies can switch the timing of their investment flows, but such changes as do take place will be in a stabilising direction.

The belief that floating rates deter long-term investment was belied by Canada's experience, as the world's leading capital importer while on a floating rate in the 1960s. A more distant example in time and space is provided by the Argentine, where foreign investment reached its peak in 1885–90 at a time of freely floating rates.[16]

Is there a case for having two floating rates, one for capital and the other for current transactions?

There is already a floating rate in the investment dollar market, which is fed by sales of British-held overseas securities, and it is through this that most non-Sterling Area overseas investment outflows are channelled. The effect of separating this rather small market from the rest of the foreign exchange market is that fluctuations in it are very much magnified. Rates for capital transactions can only differ from those on current transactions if access to the investment currency market is artificially restricted. The effect – apart from accentuating instability and providing a temptation to seek out leaks – is to put an artificial and arbitrary penalty on the use of foreign exchange for investment compared with other uses, including imports. If the Government wants to put an artificial loading against overseas investment – say on the grounds that some of the return is 'wasted' in tax payments to foreign governments – the best way of doing so would probably be by means of a general percentage tax which reflected the supposed discrepancy. A supporter of exchange rate flexibility might support a system of two floating rates as a crisis measure, or as a step away from 'fixed' rates. But the separation of the two rates would be a harmful and unnecessary distortion if allowed to persist.

To come back to forward rates for a moment. How about smaller, or underdeveloped, countries, which are unlikely to have developed foreign exchange markets?

Such countries can always deal in the forward exchange markets of one of the larger or more advanced countries, and they can trade or make contracts with each other in, or via, these currencies. Indeed there is a long tradition in the remoter areas of invoicing in dollars or European currencies.

What post-war evidence has there been of the stability or otherwise of foreign exchange markets under floating rates?

The greatest difficulty faced by advocates of floating rates is undoubtedly the sheer lack of empirical evidence, one way or the other, for advanced industrial countries in postwar conditions. The supporters of fixed rates seem extremely anxious that such evidence should not become available. When the Germans floated the mark for a short period in the autumn of 1969, every conceivable pressure was brought on them to bring the experiment to an end as soon as possible before it could yield useful data.

The German experience was of limited value because it was made clear that the authorities would soon fix another rate. The market was therefore not trying to take a view of fundamentals, but simply to guess what the German authorities might do; and plenty of hints were provided from that quarter. The rate rose fairly quickly at the end of September to a premium of near 7 per cent, in accordance with the Bundesbank's proclaimed views of where the new rate should be. Then there was a smaller climb in the last few days of the free market in

October, when there were fresh hints that the revaluation at the new rate would be slightly higher; it turned out to be just over 9 per cent.

The German experience did show, however, that the foreign exchange market can operate a floating rate without the chaos that many had predicted and without interfering with the flow of international payments. It also showed that a temporary period of floating rates can be an alternative to the 'swap' credits between central banks when currencies are under pressure. The episode will not be forgotten quickly.

The only extensive post-war experience is provided, however, by Canada from 1950 to 1961. During the whole eleven-year period the Canadian dollar stayed within the range of 93–106·2 U.S. cents. The biggest movement within a single month was $2\frac{11}{16}$ cents, and for the overwhelming majority of months the range of movement was less than 2 cents. Within a single year the range between the highest and lowest quotation was never less than $2\frac{1}{2}$ per cent or more than 6 per cent of the annual average. Up to the end of 1960, moreover, there was extremely little official intervention. Most of what did take place was of a short-term 'smoothing' variety. This can be demonstrated by the very small fluctuations in official reserve holdings, where the average monthly change was only $20 million and the maximum in a single month was no more than $100 million.

Why then did the Canadians abandon their floating rate?

They did so in circumstances which illustrate the possibility of inept government intervention rather than any shortcomings of floating exchange rates. To summarise very briefly: in the late 1950s and early 1960s Canada was suffering from a severe unemployment problem at a time when the overseas balance was composed of a current deficit offset by a capital inflow. A tight money and high interest rate policy was adopted. This kept down home demand and aggravated unemployment. It also increased the inflow of U.S. capital, which was heavily criticised on political grounds.

At a very late stage, in June 1961, Finance Minister Fleming reversed engines and embarked on a policy of fiscal and monetary expansion. Instead of just letting this new policy take its course, and allowing the exchange rate to depreciate of its own accord, the Canadian authorities embarked on a totally unnecessary policy of 'talking the rate down' combined with some intervention in the foreign exchange market in this direction. At first the market was sceptical of the Government's ability to achieve its objective, not realising the potency of the expansionary monetary policy. Suddenly the rate gave way; and partly because the market was unaware of the Government's true intentions, heavy selling pressure developed in early 1962, and the attempt of the authorities to hold the rate in the market led to a large outflow of funds. The Canadian Government responded to the crisis by devaluing the Canadian dollar in April 1962 by 2·9 per cent from the prevailing market rate to a new fixed parity of 92·5 U.S. cents. The new rate itself came under very severe pressure; by June 1962 the Canadian Government had used a third of its resources in supporting it against speculative pressures. Restrictive internal measures had to be taken, and an I.M.F. rescue operation was launched. A chain of action which had started with government concern over high unemployment thus ended with a tightening of monetary and fiscal policy to protect the new fixed rate.

The moral of the story is that a floating rate cannot itself ensure sensible domestic policies. It can merely provide an opportunity for such policies to be followed, by removing the conflict between internal and external objectives likely to exist under a fixed rate. No system is proof against a failure to take advantage of it.[17]

What is the evidence cited by those who believed that floating rates between the wars were destabilising?

The inter-war period is a particularly unhelpful one from which to seek guidance. Countries resorting to floating rates in the early 1920s as a transitional measure pending a return to a fixed gold parity, and the authorities deliberately pushed the market rate towards the parities at which they were aiming. The floating rates of the 1930s were in response to the Depression emergency. Professor Milton Friedman has several times warned of the 'Arizona effect'. Because tuberculosis sufferers go to Arizona, the death rate from that disease is higher there than anywhere else in the U.S.A., and innocent observers might regard it as the unhealthiest state. Similarly, because countries suffering from wars or depressions often adopt floating rates, it might seem that floating rates are particularly disaster-prone.

It is obviously impossible to give a potted inter-war history in this short book. But it is worth mentioning the very great influence of the interpretation given to the inter-war experience by the late Professor

Ragnar Nurkse in his 1944 League of Nations study.[18] This helped to form the view of the post-war generation of economists and officials and thereby influenced indirectly many others who had not read it themselves.

Nurkse's four main examples of the destabilising effect of exchange rates were the French inflation of the early 1920s, the U.K. experience of 1931–2, the U.S. experience after going off gold in 1933–4, and the French experience during the Popular Front Government of 1936–9. The first case will be discussed a little further on in relation to the inflation argument. The other three illustrate the consequences of a sudden abandonment of fixed parities – whether fixed by a gold link or government intervention in the foreign exchange market – after a justified speculative attack. Lack of business confidence in a 'Left-wing' government was a factor in the Popular Front example, which would have been worse if a completely pegged rate had given speculators a one-way option. The American example was a case of a beggar-my-neighbour attempt to export unemployment in a depression, when a New Deal Government was at a loss for better methods. None of these cases can provide any idea of what floating rates would be like as a continuous system in non-depression conditions when governments have ample means of maintaining home demand. Those whose opposition to floating rates is based primarily on inter-war experience should at least re-examine the Nurkse-type interpretation in the light of more recent criticisms.[19]

Can you say a little on British experience with a floating pound in the 1930s?

Conditions were so utterly different from today's that to make many inferences from them one way or the other would be an example of the 'Arizona' fallacy. But for what it is worth, three phases can be distinguished:

1. *1931–3: depression phase*

A number of countries went off overvalued gold parities. Sterling dropped from $4.87 in August 1931, when the U.K. left the gold standard, to $3.23 in December. In 1933, however, the pound climbed back to the old level against the dollar because of the U.S. departure from gold and subsequent dollar depreciation. No one would argue that a period of severe depression which countries entered with fixed rates of exchange which they then had to abandon, because they ceased to work altogether, provides good evidence about floating rates as a normal continuing system.

2. *1934 to early 1938*

This may be a slightly more relevant period. The U.K. then had a floating but highly managed pound. The Exchange Equalisation Account intervened in the market to keep the rate steady but not rigid, and the system worked without an official par value. Central banks co-operated to 'stabilise' the market. This co-operation was formalised by the Tripartite Agreement of 1936 between the U.S.A., Britain and France, which followed the French departure from their gold parity. This declared (in terms reminiscent of post-war 'Basle' declarations) 'the intention of the three governments to continue to use the appropriate available resources as well as to avoid as far as possible any disturbance of the basis of international exchanges resulting from the proposed readjustment.'

Advocates of floating rates might argue that the Bank of England erred too much in the direction of rigidity. The value of the Bank of England's gold reserve, including the holdings of the Exchange Equalisation Account, increased from £121 million in 1932 to £840 million in March 1938. Only a small part of this was due to the rise in the sterling price of gold. The bulk of the increase represented a deliberate policy of preventing the appreciation of sterling. A case could be made for this policy, as the tendency to appreciate was largely due to the inflow of politically motivated 'refugee capital' from the Continent, which was liable to be withdrawn if war risks increased. The value of the absence of an official par value was that, if conditions changed, the Bank knew that it could let the rate move in either direction without the political hurdle of a formal devaluation or revaluation.

3. *1938–9*

From February 1938 adverse international political and other pressures did indeed develop. The rate slid back from a high point of \$5.02 to a low of \$4.67 in the early winter of 1938–9. Temporary stability was then reached. Fresh war pressures afterwards pulled the rate down, until it reached \$4.27 at the end of August. In September 1939 the rate was pegged at \$4.02. Even in the immediate pre-war period the fluctuations were thus not wild. The 1938 slide, for instance, was a good deal less than any of the post-war devaluations and, of course, more gradual.

The experience of 1931–3 is as much an object lesson in the folly of sticking to overvalued fixed rates for too long as it is to floating rates. From then onwards there was nothing to suggest that foreign exchange markets were any more unstable than they would have been with a par value system. A Chatham House Report by H. W. Arndt, *The Economic Lessons of the 1930s*,[20] published at the same time as the Nurkse study, remarks: 'There can be little doubt that the abandonment of the gold standard and the depreciation of the pound, which were generally considered at the time as a disaster of the first magnitude, constituted in fact the first important step towards helping Great Britain out of the depression.' But the main difference between the 1930s and today surely is that in the former period governments could think of no better way of coping with slumps than by exporting their unemployment problem; and central bank co-operation was partly devoted to bringing about a truce in such beggar-my-neighbour activities. Today governments know perfectly well how to stimulate demand and mop up excess unemployment by internal financial expansion (unless they are prevented from doing so by fixed exchange rates). The more usual problem is to prevent them pushing expansion too far.

How disturbing have floating rates been to international trade in the past?

If one examines the experience of a number of European countries in the 1920s, there is no acceleration or any other notable break in the trend of trade volumes following the return to fixed gold parities. Even in the early 1930s, there is some evidence that the trade of countries on floating rates, depressed though it was, declined less than that of countries which remained pegged to gold.

The period of 1846–80, that of Cobden and Bright, was the heyday of free trade and also an era of active international lending. Yet, contrary to popular belief, it was to some extent an era of fluctuating exchange rates. The U.S.A. had an irredeemable 'greenback' currency, floating against the rest of the world from the Civil War in the early 1860s to 1879. U.S. export and import volumes were actually higher in relation to the G.N.P. (nearly $14\frac{1}{2}$ per cent) during the 'greenback' period than in subsequent decades (when they fell to 12–13 per cent). Austria and Russia were frequently on inconvertible paper standards after the

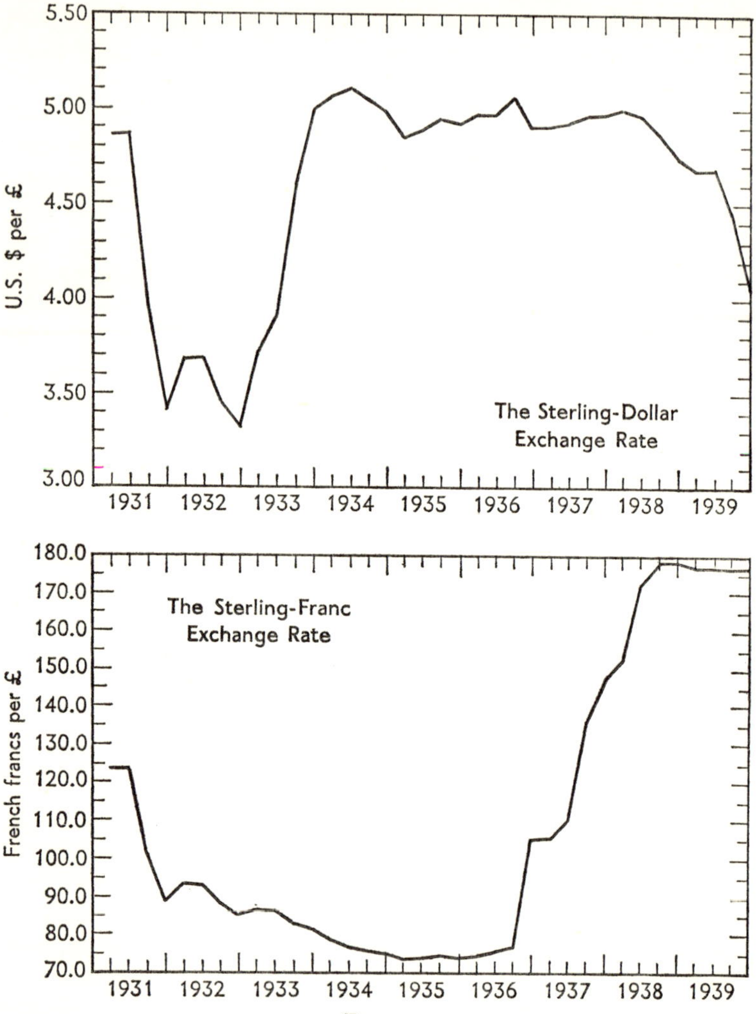

FIG. 2

Exchange Rates in the 1930s (Figures are weekly averages for ends of quarters). Source: Bank of England.

middle of the nineteenth century. ('Inconvertible' means inconvertible into gold by the authorities at a fixed rate; it does not imply exchange controls of the twentieth-century type.)

Exchange rates between countries on gold and silver standards were originally linked by France's 'bimetallic' policy of dealing in both metals at a fixed $15\frac{1}{2}$ to 1 ratio. As a result of the silver glut of the 1870s the French abandoned this policy, and currencies on silver standards depreciated against those on gold currencies. (This was the background to Miss Prism's remark in *The Importance of Being Earnest*: 'The Chapter on the Fall of the Rupee you may omit. It is somewhat too sensational for a young girl. Even these metallic problems have their melodramatic side.') Yet such events did not prevent a rapid growth of trade between gold, silver and paper-standard countries. The growth of world trade was if anything slightly lower in the twenty years up to 1914, when a genuine international gold standard did exist, than in the previous half-century when it did not.

None of this is offered as more than negative evidence that floating exchange rates need not have the disruptive effects on trade so often alleged. Perhaps the least irrelevant episode is that of Canada, which had a floating rate from 1950 to 1961. Canada's share of world trade measured in U.S. dollars was if anything slightly higher during that decade than before and afterwards. Of course other forces were at work too, and the only point worth making is that a fluctuating rate did not prevent Canada from enjoying a fairly stable 5–6 per cent share in world trade.[21]

Does not a floating exchange rate remove the main restraint on inflation – the fear of a payments deficit?

The arguments cut both ways. The difficulty of adjusting the exchange rate does put *some* discipline on governments in a deficit country, but it is very imperfect and diluted. Under a 'fixed' rate, there is a series of lags between the initial pumping of excessive purchasing power into the economy, the resultant domestic overheating and wage inflation, the payments deficit, and the eventual foreign exchange crises. The process is longer and more difficult for the public to grasp than the fall in a free-market exchange rate. The latter is an immediate index of failure, which affects the retail price index and which all can follow.

One cannot be sure which set of influences is the more powerful. 'Fixed' exchange rates have not been conspicuously successful in stopping inflation in the last few years. When all countries are increasing their prices simultaneously, the 'discipline' of a fixed rate is simply to conform to the world average. In surplus countries, they are actually an incentive to more rapid inflation. Sermons about pricing ourselves out of world markets carry less and less conviction each time the threatened horrors fail to materialise. Under a floating rate the real arguments against inflation – the internal ones – will replace the external bogey, and the public will be able to judge the issue in the most transparent and least technical form possible.

Even if the above analysis is wrong, and floating exchange rates are marginally more inflationary than the adjustable peg, it is still questionable whether officials and central bankers should not misuse their role as technical advisers to advise Ministers against floating rates purely for the purpose of 'disciplining' them. Representative democracy has many faults, and there may be a case for imposing some checks and balances. But are Treasury officials and central bankers the right people to exercise the functions of a second chamber?

The inflationary arguments in any case do not apply to surplus countries whose currencies would float upwards. Nor do they apply to schemes for 'discretionary upward crawl' of the kind advocated by Dr Emminger of the Bundesbank and Dr Zijlstra of the Netherlands Bank. The most anti-inflationary payments mechanism would in fact be a floating rate with a lower, but no upper, limit, with the floor itself being moved up towards the market rate from time to time. The inflationary argument is, however, so finely balanced that there is an overwhelming case for flexibility in both directions for the sake of ending the balance of payments obsession.

The real danger is not that of governments embarking on consciously inflationary policies. Any chance or speculative movement that depresses the exchange rate will push up the price level and trigger off a chain of wage increases. In this way the original speculative movement will prove self-justifying and the currency will have embarked on a rake's progress.

It is worth remembering at the outset that slightly less than a fifth of all U.K. expenditure is devoted to imports, directly or indirectly. Even if all exchange rate changes were completely passed on in import prices, it would take a plunge of well over 10 per cent in the rate to have as much influence as a 2 per cent acceleration in the rise of domestic costs.

The question arises as to why the rate should drop. If it is because of some incipient payments deficit, then the initial increase in import prices helps to bring about the check to the growth of home spending that will in any case be necessary under conditions of near-full employment. It is up to the Government to carry out a fiscal and monetary policy to ensure that incomes do not rise faster in an attempt to avoid this check. If the Government lacks the political will or strength to do so, no other method of adjustment, whether devaluation, import controls, or any other, will succeed. (This is discussed further in the 'answer' on p. 67.)

If – and this is what lies behind the question – the exchange rate movement is larger than justified by fundamental forces, the authorities can throw some of their own reserves on the market, or borrow from overseas, to put a brake on the fall in the rate. Such intervention of course assumes that the authorities have a better idea of 'fundamental' forces than the foreign exchange market.

Were there not phases in the German, Austrian and French inflations after the First World War when the rate of exchange depreciation exceeded the rate of increase of the price level or of the money supply?

Yes. These and similar experiences led a whole generation to suppose that floating exchange rates could be an independent cause of currency collapse. But received interpretations are often incorrect. Leads and lags of this kind prove little about cause and effect. The real question to ask is what would have happened if the money supply *and* the domestic budgets had been stabilised in these countries. It is surely likely that their exchange rates would also have ceased tumbling downwards. On the other hand, if the exchange rate had been frozen, but the money supply had continued to shoot upwards and large budget deficits continued unchecked, is it likely that inflation would have stopped? On the contrary, the exchange rate itself would have given way again or would have had to be supported with foreign loans. It is because the foreign exchange market is such a sensitive indicator that it registers at an early stage market anticipations about inflation. In the cases cited, the markets had ample justification in predicting an acceleration of inflation. This sensitivity was heightened in the German case when the Government obtained hard currency for reparations by printing marks and selling them on the foreign exchange market!

Can you think of situations where a Government would be likely to have a better idea of fundamental forces than the foreign exchange market?

Let us suppose that a Government has a weak record and had been unable or unwilling to control the budget and/or money supply; and that this history has given rise to highly inflationary expectations. If there is now a change of direction, the new reformed policy is quite likely to run into a credibility gap – especially if the extent of the change has been hidden by the Byzantine complexities of the British fiscal and monetary system. Yet it is in just such a situation that a Government is most likely to be approaching the exhaustion of its reserves and its ability or willingness to borrow overseas.

The above is a thumbnail sketch of the British situation in the first half of 1969. This would clearly not have been the best time to float the pound, but it is in just such situations that countries are most likely to be forced to do so – as the U.K. was planning to do if evidence of recovery had been delayed even a few months longer.

Another example was after the French wage explosion of May 1968. The willingness of the French Government, with support from the I.M.F. and central banks, to allow the balance of payments to move into deficit, together with temporary price controls, prevented the real value of the wage increases from being eroded as quickly as would have otherwise happened. Although these moves could bring little permanent gain to French workers, they did buy time at a particularly dangerous moment, and allowed the readjustment to be postponed until the return of political stability. If France had been on a floating rate, a similar effect could have been obtained by official intervention in the foreign exchange market with the aid of precisely the same sources of international finance. But given the previously existing pegged rate, May 1968 was hardly the ideal time to let go of the peg.

When then would be the ideal time for the U.K. to float?

The ideal time would be when the balance of payments is in surplus and the figures give if anything too favourable, rather than too gloomy, an impression, when confidence is fairly high and debts are being repaid and when inflationary expectations are no worse than in other countries. In these conditions a big depreciation is most unlikely, and the floating rate can be seen as a long-term regulator rather than as an emergency expedient. One such situation was in the winter of 1966–7, when there was a freak basic surplus in the final quarter of 1966 amounting to over £600 million per annum and all central bank assistance was repaid. An even better time would indeed have been very early on in the spring of 1970 – better because the surplus then was not so completely freakish. But it is in just such situations that governments can claim that their policies are at last 'working' and are least likely to undertake experiments. Those Ministers and officials whose main argument against floating the rate up to the middle of 1969 was a blood-curdling prediction of what would happen if the rate would fall, did not abate their opposition when this fear ceased to carry any plausibility.

What other measures would have to accompany a British decision to float?

If there is no threat of 'overheating' or payments deficit at the time of the decision, there would be no need for any dramatic change in short-term policy. But the more the authorities can make their longer-term intentions clear, the more stable the foreign exchange market is likely to be. The most important single announcement would be about the pace of I.M.F. and other debt repayment and any target for reserve rebuilding. At present, debt repayment is for practical purposes made at the rate at which foreign exchange flows back to London. Under a floating rate the timing would be a matter of deliberate choice and government purchases of foreign exchange would be one of the most important influences on the rate; the market would therefore need to know the authorities' intentions at least in outline. Other necessary announcements would have to cover the future of the investment currency dollar, the overseas investment restrictions, and exchange control generally. One suggestion might be a timetable announcing a phased return to freedom. It would also be highly desirable to indicate the authorities' present thinking on the future of the Basle arrangements for sterling. This would also be a good occasion for announcing long-term policy on tariffs. Money supply policy has already been mentioned. Obviously a decision to float would have many more detailed technical implications, which would have to be clarified. But the above is enough to show that a 'dash for freedom' itself requires careful planning.

What kind of internal financial policy would a permanent system of floating rates require?

A floating rate can help to banish pseudo-problems. But it is no magic wand and will only work satisfactorily if backed by sensible internal policies. If the exchange rate is moving downwards, 'room' will have to be made for a diversion of resources to exports and import-saving. If the currency is appreciating, to remove a surplus, domestic demand will have to be allowed to rise unless – as in Germany in 1969 – the economy is starting from a seriously overheated position.

The basic difficulty about a floating rate is that, in contrast to all alternatives, it is almost too good at keeping overseas payments in balance. Under a fixed rate, if too much demand is allowed to build up, the deterioration in the overseas deficit is a safety valve. The safety valve allows in extra resources from overseas which help to counteract inflationary pressures. A freely fluctuating rate, on the other hand, will normally fall to whatever level is required to secure balance. If home demand is excessive, the fall could be severe and the inflationary consequences serious. Thus while a freely fluctuating rate would enable governments to dispense with mistimed intervention of a stop–go character, it would become even more important to avoid domestic overheating. As errors are inevitable in economic management, Governments would have to be relatively modest in the target pressure of demand at which they aimed.

The above is inevitably on a high plane of generality. Despite the arguments between the devotees of monetary and fiscal policy, there is a considerable store of detailed knowledge and experience about how to preserve a given parity or make a devaluation work. By contrast, the working rules for an internal policy to accompany a floating rate do not yet exist – and inevitably so, given the lack of post-war experience from which to generalise, and the lack of incentive for officials and research institutions to make the necessary studies. It is no service to the cause of exchange rate flexibility to hide this fact.

The above is not an argument against moving to floating rates. A man will never learn the finer points of driving if he refuses to take the wheel. It is, however, an argument for some 'fail-safe' device. Much the best check – because it would in any case be desirable – would be to put a definite limit on both the long-term growth of the money supply and the size of the public-sector deficit at full employment. The actual monetary growth in a particular year might all within a target range, and if by bad luck or bad management the limit were exceeded in any one year, there would have to be a corresponding retardation in years to come. To rely on short-term economic forecasts alone without such long-term guidelines would be too dangerous. In the absence of a long-term control of the growth of the money supply and the fiscal balance, I would be much more doubtful of the case for a freely fluctuating rate and would prefer to go for one of the compromise schemes for limited flexibility.

With the budget and money supply under control, it is, however, extremely unlikely that the spiral of cumulative depreciation and inflation, feared by the anti-floaters, could occur. This view does not depend on any exaggerated belief in the short-term effectiveness of monetary policy or in any desire to abandon fiscal regulators.[22] It depends only on the assumption that there are long-run limits to the velocity of circulation. On the older definition, for which historical series exist, the velocity of circulation has stayed within the range of 2–3 from the 1870s to the present day. An exception to this statement was the Depression years of the 1930s and the immediate war and post-war period of ultra-cheap money when it fell to $1\frac{1}{3}$,[23] (Velocity is defined as the ratio of the national income to the quantity of money at any given time. If the growth of the money supply is reasonably even over a period of years and not too much larger than the trend growth of output, there is most unlikely to be a runaway inflation, whatever short-term fluctuations take place in the foreign exchange market. If in addition the Government keeps a close control over the budget deficit (suitably defined on a 'full employment' basis), this statement can be made with all the more confidence.

Surely the real worry about floating rates is that it takes time – say a year or two – for an exchange rate change to affect the current balance of payments? If the exchange rate depreciates, the initial effect may be to make a deficit worse – the dollar prices of British goods are likely to go down, long before there is a compensating increase in sales volume.

The adverse initial response of the current balance to exchange depreciation, followed by an eventual and larger improvement, is known as the '*J*-curve'. It is probably the biggest single objection of Whitehall economists to floating rates. But it arises from ignoring capital movement. Currency holders will take a view of the longer-term equilibrium rate and will, in their own interest, support the market at that level and provide the temporary finance required. If the authorities think they know the ultimate level better than the market, they can – if necessary with I.M.F. or central bank support – make 'stabilising' purchases of foreign exchange themselves. This is exactly what happens at present after a devaluation; the difference is that under a floating rate the authorities are not committed for the next few years to their initial guess about the right rate, but can change their support point in the light of further knowledge and experience.

How much intervention by the authorities would you personally favour?

There is a great deal to be said for keeping it to a minimum, and confining major intervention to those few rare cases where the Government may really have better knowledge than the market. An example might be a Middle East crisis, where the Government may have military or political information enabling it to take a less alarmist view and may also have better knowledge of its own political intentions. (The pre-war case cited on p. 58 was another example.) A more debatable example would be a pensions increase which the foreign exchange market regarded as more inflationary than it really was through a misunderstanding of the complexities of British social security finance.

The general argument for relying on market forces is (*a*) that those who operate in the market have their own money at stake and have the most powerful of all incentives to make the best guesses, and (*b*) that the diversity of views and range of information that influence a market are less likely to lead to a really large misjudgement than an attempt to impose the view of one group of people at the top.

Official and independent economic forecasts will, of course, still be available on a free foreign exchange market. (They will change their form slightly. The balance on official settlements will – apart from intervention or debt repayment – normally be zero, and forecasters will have to concentrate on guessing (*a*) the exchange rate and (*b*) the component items.) There is no reason why a free market should work on a hunch alone, and if economic forecasts turn out to be useful, they will influence market rates.

Does not the international position of sterling nevertheless rule out a floating rate?

The view that sterling's international role made it impossible for the currency to float was always a dubious one. Overseas holders of a currency are likely to withdraw their funds when they believe that the currency is more likely to depreciate than appreciate – a situation characteristic of a fixed rate under pressure. The reason why official Sterling Area holders became restless after the 1967 devaluation was because they thought a second devaluation was a real possibility, while an appreciation of the pound was not.

But there have been so many changes since 1967 that there is no need to pursue the argument in its traditional form. It was often said that either a devaluation or a move to a floating rate by sterling would trigger off a run on the dollar with dire risks for the world monetary system. Since the adoption of the two-tier gold price in March 1968, an old-fashioned run on the dollar can no longer take place. As the result of the separation of the official and private gold markets, there is no possibility of a drain of official gold stocks draining off into private hands. In addition, the Basle arrangements of September 1968 – under which Sterling Area authorities agreed not to run down the sterling proportion of their reserves, in exchange for a guarantee of their dollar value – ought to mean the end of the old sterling balance worry.

The desirability of retaining freedom to vary the exchange rate is the most important single reason for not letting the Basle arrangements just run out after 1971, even if sterling appears strong at the time, but to renegotiate them on a permanent rather than an *ad hoc* basis. The arrangements have been a brilliant success. All the official balances that had been withdrawn after devaluation were returned to London in 1968–9 long before there was any evidence that Britain's own balance of payments had moved into surplus.

This success is not really surprising, as overseas Sterling Area holders have been compensated for any devaluation risk twice over. They have enjoyed a capital guarantee, but have still received a competitive interest rate which itself reflects the risk premium demanded by non-guaranteed sterling holders. This feature resulting from the panicky atmosphere of 1968 should be amended in any renegotiation. One suggestion made by Professor B. Cohen is that Sterling Area members should, in return for the exchange guarantee, be obliged to invest a proportion of their sterling balances in special non-interest-bearing securities – the proportion perhaps to be related to the difference between representative interest rates in London and New York.[24] Even more important is his suggestion that the renegotiated facility should be available to offset withdrawals of *private as well as official* balances, both inside and outside the Sterling Area. These have in practice proved the most volatile section of the balances, and optional funding of these at the discretion of the holders would be much less expensive for Britain than the wholesale funding advocated in some of the more ambitious plans for reform.

Another myth is that the City of London's overseas earnings depend on a fixed exchange rate. Less is heard of this than formerly. If such exchange earnings could continue to flourish after a sudden devaluation in defiance of the most solemn pledges to sterling holders, it is likely that they could survive a gradually moving sterling rate. The most volatile of the gross private sterling balances – £500 million in all – were run down in the five years up to the end of 1968. While some rebuilding of balances is likely and natural, any funds which were deposited in London in the belief that the parity could never change have fortunately gone for good. Moreover, interest paid on overseas balances is a debit item in the current balance of payments, a relevant fact that is often glossed over.

The greater part of the City's net invisible overseas earnings consists of services such as shipping and insurance which are in no way dependent on sterling being an international currency. Nor is this all. Despite the public utterances of City spokesmen, the financial institutions themselves have adapted themselves to the decline of sterling's international role by switching borrowing and lending operations to overseas currencies and particulary to Euro-dollars. Thus, as Table 5 shows, there has been anything but a decline, even on the banking side.

Table 5
NET OVERSEAS EARNINGS OF U.K. FINANCIAL INSTITUTIONS

	1965	*1966*	*1967*	*1968*
		£m.		
Insurance* (including portfolio income)	49	77	111	139
Investment trusts, etc.	35	37	37	48
Miscellaneous brokerage†	28	27	31	42
Merchanting profit	30–35	30–35	30–35	30–35
Banking	32	16	19	40

* Excluding U.K. earnings of overseas insurers.
† Including non-commodity earnings of Baltic Exchange, Stock Exchange, Lloyds Register of Shipping, commissions of bullion dealers and overseas fees for portfolio management.
Source: *U.K. Balance of Payments*, 1969, Appendix 5.

The banking item is of course the difference between much larger gross credit and debit items, amounting in 1968 to £152 million and £112 million respectively.

Many of the above activities are, of course, hampered by extremely severe exchange control and overseas investment restrictions, which could more easily be relaxed or abandoned for good under a floating rate. Under such a regime, one might even look forward to some revival in sterling's role as a *trading* currency if that were regarded as desirable object of policy.

It is all very well if one country floats; but how would trade be carried out and prices quoted, if every currency floated against every other?

There is no insuperable problem here. When prices of different commodities fluctuate against each other, money is used as a common measuring rod. Similarly if currencies float against each other, one particular currency would be used as a yardstick. This might be the most important currency, or the most stable currency, or the one of which the most 'bullish' view is taken. Alternatively if one major currency retained a gold link under a floating system, other currencies might be quoted against it. For the foreseeable future there is no doubt that the dollar would remain the most widely used yardstick, although there would also be regional yardsticks based on other currencies in certain parts of the world. Indeed this already happens at the moment.

It would clearly ease the transition to a floating rate system, and accustom people to the mechanics, if one or two countries made the experiment first and others joined later. The view that the transition can only be safely made as part of an international agreement affecting all currencies is the opposite of the truth. Confidential discussions to secure acceptance and avoid misunderstandings between any country contemplating such a step and the key figures in the I.M.F. and Group of Ten would be highly desirable. The I.M.F. itself might even want to encourage a particular Government to make an experiment in flexibility (see p. 88.) But this is all very different from expecting the whole world to make the change in a common step.

If you are going to have a floating exchange rate, why stop at existing state frontiers? Why should there not be a floating exchange rate for Scotland, or London, or Rutland Gate?

This brings one to the question of the size of an optimum currency area. Regions such as Scotland or Wales might gain some advantages in coping with their unemployment problems, by being able to depreciate against England and thereby being able to capture more orders and attract more investment. As against this, such areas would lose the undoubted advantages of an area with common money, in which the question of an exchange rate does not arise. An optimum currency area is somewhere between one's own street and the whole world. Exactly what it is, is probably the most interesting, and unsolved, question in the whole exchange rate issue.

It is unrealistic to speak as if every currency were likely to float against every other. Small countries would be likely to adhere to larger neighbours, and formal and informal currency blocs would emerge. The peripheral countries would be under no illusions about the fixity of their own centre's currency against other key currencies, and the feelings of bad faith which accompanied the devaluation of the pound in the Sterling Area could not arise.

In such a world, the currency centres could not suffer from balance of payments problems, provided they did not grant gold convertibility for official overseas balances. The onus would be on the peripheral countries, when in surplus, to decide whether to hold excess supplies of the centre's currency or allow their own currencies to appreciate and abandon the link – exactly the same problem that faces the rest of the world in relation to the dollar. A worse problem would be faced by the peripheral countries in potential deficit. To maintain the link, they would either have to gear their financial policies to those of the centre, or be prepared to impose restrictions on trade and payments, which would destroy many of the advantages of having the link. If the British pound floated, and the Irish pound maintained its sterling link, the U.K. would not have to worry about its balance of payments. But the Irish authorities would run out of sterling with which to support the Irish pound in the market if they were imprudent in their policies.

These are examples of a proposition which is blindingly obvious once it is stated. This is that the authorities of surplus countries can either hold the currencies they acquire or sell them (or lend them out on the Euro-dollar Market.) Once the authorities of the deficit, or potentially deficit, countries cease to worry about maintaining a given exchange rate, the onus of decision falls on the surplus countries; and this automatically removes the bias in the present system under which nearly the whole task of adjustment has fallen on the deficit countries. A deficit country cannot float against the wishes of its trading partners, but it can force them to choose between allowing it to float and indefinite financing of its deficits.

Several criteria have been suggested for an optimum currency area, members of which would hold their exchange rates constant. One is mobility of factors of production such as labour and capital. If there is a fall in English demand for Scottish goods, Scottish workers can move south, or English capital move north to employ the surplus labour in alternative industries – not with perfect ease or we would not have regional problems, but much more easily than, say, between the U.K. and Japan.

A second criterion is the proportion of traded to non-traded goods. Let us assume that an area with a payments deficit exports the whole of its production in exchange for imports and is in deficit. Then a demand-reducing policy will affect only the import bill; there will be no unemployment or waste of resources and there is no point in exchange depreciation as a complementary weapon. On the other hand, if the trade sector is a small part of the total (and wages and prices are not flexible downwards), then a demand-reducing policy will, if pushed beyond a certain point, reduce output and employment by a multiple of the saving in imports, and the ability of the area to reduce its exchange rate can prevent such a waste of resources.

The trouble with such criteria is (*a*) that they contain no numbers (how large is 'large'?), and (*b*) that they assume that one is able to start dividing the world up from scratch. In fact there is a great deal to be said for treating at least the larger sovereign industrial states as separate currency areas. The point has already been made that Scotland loses the freedom to vary its exchange rate, but in return has the advantage of belonging to a single capital market and trading area within which custom barriers of any kind are inconceivable, and obtains fiscal and other assistance from the more prosperous regions. No such bargains exist between, say, the U.K. and Germany.

If one wants to move beyond the nation's state to wider areas, national policies and traditions must be taken into account. It would make no sense to treat a country like France, with a record of inflation and devaluation, and one like Germany with a record of relative price stability and appreciation, as an optimum currency area, despite their mutual trade, and a premature attempt in this direction of the kind under discussion in Brussels will impede rather than help the free movement of trade and payments within the European Community.

Is not the campaign for floating rates basically a nationalist backlash, by those who wish to pursue policies independent of the rest of the world? Would it not be more constructive to develop international co-operation, to a point where exchange rate changes become no longer necessary?

Neither national nor international government is an end in itself. All governmental agencies from the parish council to the I.M.F. or the E.E.C. Commission are to be judged by their effects on the welfare of individuals whose lives they influence. Different sized units are suitable for different purposes. For some purposes the existing national states may be too large, for others too small. Because a world authority with a monopoly of military (or at least nuclear) force would be desirable, it does not follow that there ought to be a world monetary authority to co-ordinate policies with the object of maintaining exchange rates. Indeed a world federal government might rationally decide to allow separate currency areas linked by flexible exchange rates, as a deliberate matter of policy. Co-ordination, it is often forgotten, can be brought about through the market, as well as by meetings of Ministers and officials.

Let us, however, assume for the sake of argument that the world – or at least the developed Western world – is an optimum currency area, in the sense that if one were starting afresh there would be a single currency throughout the area, with no restrictions on trade and payments. International companies tend automatically to support this view, and irrespective of whether it is a theoretical optimum or not, the prospect must hold many attractions to any liberal. It would be a realisation of Cobden's dream, and in the heyday of the international gold standard the world seemed to be going in that direction.

One sign that a world currency area existed, would surely be the complete absence of balance of payments problems. A payments disequilibrium between Germany and France would be no more likely to arise than between Yorkshire and Lancashire or the provinces of the Roman Empire. Adjustments would take place through transfers of money between areas, without the aid of governments, as described by David Hume 200 years ago. Hume was, of course, writing about a world in which gold was the normal form of money. In a world of paper money, a common currency area would require (*a*) *immutability* of exchange rates, and (*b*) complete convertibility assured at all times. A world currency area could have a single form of money supplied by a world central bank. Alternatively, there could be several central banks issuing individual currencies rigidly linked in the way described. Each central bank would, however, have very little freedom of policy and would have to conform to the world average. The two variants would seem very similar from the point of view of individuals and firms.

But the second would be inferior as there would be no conscious control of the world money supply.[25]

Under floating rates too there could be no balance of payments problems, and no need to impose restrictions on trade and payments, as exchange rate variations would take the place of currency transfers. *Both systems thus have much more in common with each other than either has with the present system of independent national paper currencies linked through pegged but ultimately adjustable exchange rates.* Under the latter system, balance of payments problems and runs on currencies are endemic, and give rise to the familiar crises and restrictions.

Internationalist supporters of fixed exchange rates confuse ends with means. The best way to approach a 'one-world economy' would be (*a*) to abolish the balance of payments problem by moving to floating rates, (*b*) to remove tariffs and other restrictions on trade and payments, and (*c*) to reduce the need for exchange rate movement by a gradual harmonisation of policies so that underlying conditions required smaller parity changes. To attempt to peg exchange rate changes when such harmonisation is still a distant hope leads only to investment and travel restrictions, exchange control, back-door export subsidies, distrust of the weaker currencies and – in the end – sudden jumps in the exchange rate. It is thus a bogus form of internationalism.

Whatever might be ideally desirable, floating rates would be 'managed' by governments and central banks. How much stability would there really be in a foreign exchange market in which national authorities were intervening frequently and extensively?

It would be better if national authorities did not intervene except for short-term smoothing, or in the kind of emergency discussed on p.68. Unfortunately, it is extremely unlikely that governments could be relied upon to exercise this self-restraint; and once national authorities engage in buying and selling currencies, the situation becomes one of oligopoly rather than competition, and consultation is required to prevent competitive depreciation or other forms of currency warfare.

Such problems are not avoided under the present system, when international soundings are still required to make sure that devaluations are not offset by matching moves elsewhere. If one or more countries floated, exchange rates would probably become an extra instrument to be discussed, along with fiscal and monetary policy and 'swaps', by bodies such as O.E.C.D.'s 'Working Party Three' and the central bankers' monthly Basle meetings. Exchange rates might well be 'stabilised' by central banks for longer than many economists would desire. But changes, when they did occur, would take on much more the appearance of small technical shifts in market tactics. This would be in sharp contract to the present situation when highly-charged political decisions have to be made about major revaluations or devaluations. Parity changes would almost certainly be smaller, more frequent, and more easily reversible. After all, oligopolists in national markets dislike price competition and prefer stability; yet one way or another, prices do gradually change over the years. But perhaps the biggest advantage of all in a floating system is that, as already mentioned, the onus is on the creditor country to decide whether or not to allow its exchange rate to appreciate. The debtor country need only worry about its own internal stability.

Would there not be a tendency under floating rates for international contracts to be made in terms of the strongest currency? And would not this in turn tend to eliminate the weaker currencies?

So-called 'fixed exchange rates' have not prevented a growing tendency to make international contracts and settle international transactions in a handful of major currencies. The dollar is here most notable, although sterling is still of considerable (though decreasing) importance, while other currencies, notably the mark and the yen, are coming more and more into use. Even if floating rates would accelerate this tendency, it is worth accepting to get rid of the balance of payments obsession here and now. Indeed this may be one of the ways in which the more unified world monetary system, desired by the internationalists, could come into existence.

It is in fact extremely unlikely that one currency will drive out all the others, even for international purposes, in the foreseeable future. For some purposes the most widely used currency in the area in question will predominate, for some the one most likely to appreciate in the long run, and for others the one expected to be most stable in real purchasing power. Nor are the smaller or weaker currencies likely to be eliminated altogether. One can easily envisage a world in which international currencies circulated side by side with local currencies, which would be standing at variable premia or discounts. Local currencies, subject to 'debasement', existed side by side with international currencies such as the dinar, florin, ducat, guilder and pound for the greater part of the last two thousand years. As Sir John Hicks justly remarks, 'on such a time scale as this, the U.S. dollar hardly counts".[26]

The internationalisation of the dollar does not prevent European governments from imposing any restrictions they wish on U.S. investment on nationalist grounds, any more than the use of the pound sterling in Ireland gives the British Government power over Irish policy towards overseas capital. The willingness of the world's traders and bankers to amass more dollars per annum than of any other currency does, however, increase the real spending power and share of world resources available to the Americans. In other words they are able to gain 'seignorage', which can be defined as 'the net value of resources accruing to the issuers of money'.[27] (This is shown by the U.S.A.'s ability to run a 'liquidity deficit' in its balance of payments without necessarily having always to pay fully competitive commercial rates on dollar balances.)

The issue of Special Drawing Rights will reduce American gains from seignorage only if it is accompanied by a reduction in the U.S. payments deficit. (If it is used to finance an increase in that deficit, American seignorage gains will actually be increased.) Such a reduction can only be enforced if the creditor countries are prepared, if necessary, to allow their own currencies to appreciate against the dollar. These considerations explain (*a*) the lectures given by Continental central bankers to the Americans to stop inflation, (*b*) their initial reluctance to go full steam ahead on S.D.R.s without some signs of a reduction in the U.S. deficit, and (*c*) their more recent advocacy of upward flexibility for their own currencies.

Disciplines of this kind can limit the use of the dollar as an official currency. By holding out the prospect of appreciation of other currencies, they may even slightly lessen the attractions of the dollar for trading and commercial banking purposes. But they are hardly likely to eliminate the very great attractions of the U.S. currency for these latter purposes. The only way to make serious inroads on the use of the dollar in international business would be to set up a European currency of comparable attraction. But here again, means and ends are easily confused. A European currency would have to emerge from a gradual convergence of policies and conditions, which would ultimately lessen the need for exchange rate adjustments. It is possible to pay too high a price in a probably unsuccessful attempt to reduce too quickly the seignorage gains accruing to the Americans. (The issue is discussed further on pp. 73–5 and 84–8.)

How could the dollar float?

If all other currencies floated against the dollar, the exchange rate for the dollar would be automatically fixed by the rest of the world. Under the present (adjustable peg) system the exchange rate for the dollar is also determined by the parity decisions of other countries. Just as there can only be one exchange rate between two currencies, in a world of *n* currencies there can only be $n - 1$ exchange rates. The dollar is likely to be this *n*th currency. This should be a relief rather than an anxiety to the United States. Let us assume that the U.S. prices itself out of world markets and the rest of the world is in surplus with the United States. This will lead to an outflow of dollars which will gravitate to the main surplus countries. The latter have the option of either holding the dollars and thus financing whatever deficit the U.S. produces, or selling the dollars and allowing their own currencies to appreciate.

Either way the U.S.A. has no reason to be alarmed. In a freely floating system without Government intervention, these surplus dollars would automatically come on to the market and all currencies would float against the dollar at a rate which eliminated any U.S. deficit on official settlements. The only cause for complaint by the Americans under 'managed floating' would be abrupt changes of policy by creditor countries in the amount of dollars they were willing to hold. Questions such as these would have to be discussed in bodies such as O.E.C.D.'s 'Working Party Three,' the Group of Ten and the monthly meetings of the Bank of International Settlements in Basle.

8 Sliding Parities, the E.E.C. and the Outlook

Compromise schemes, which have been summarised in Chapter 2, exist which would allow parities to move but limit the maximum movement to a moderate amount – say 2 or 3 per cent – in any particular year. These have the following advantages:

(1) They can be supported by a fairly strong body of opinion which sees the absurdity of artificially created balance of payments problems due to wrongly valued currencies and appreciates the advantages of gradual adjustment, but which does not share the belief expressed in the preceding pages in the ability of the market to arrive at the right exchange rate.

(2) Such compromise schemes can also be advocated by fully-fledged floaters as a way of accustoming people to the idea of small and gradual changes in exchange rates and demonstrating that flexibility need not mean wild fluctuations. They would hope that after a period of sliding parities opinion might be ready to take a further step forward. But even if it were not, something valuable would have been gained.

(3) Thirdly, the sliding parity seems tailor-made for areas such as the E.E.C. or other would-be currency blocs, which are trying to unify economic conditions, but are not yet anywhere near their goal. The proposal would limit fluctuation within the area and secure a fair degree of stability, without ossifying the exchange rate structure altogether.

A compromise of this kind would still involve balance of payments sanctions for countries that inflated too fast in relation to the rest of the world. But the subordination of every other object for the sake of the exchange rate for many years at a time would no longer be necessary, and a country which developed a deficit would know that exchange rate movements would, if allowed to, in time re-establish equilibrium. In the meantime speculative movements of 'hot money' could be counteracted by raising interest rates by modest amounts corresponding to the permitted exchange rate movement (or in appropriate conditions by official intervention in the forward markets.) The genuine difficulties arise not from the flexible, but from the rigid, elements in the suggested compromise. Discussing such schemes at the I.M.F. in 1969, Mr Roy Jenkins said that it would be difficult to diagnose a small disequilibrium until too late. But in situations such as the U.K. in the early 1960s, when there would have been genuine intellectual uncertainty about the need for a substantial devaluation, the benefit of the doubt would undoubtedly have been given to gradual and reversible downward adjustments.

Sliding parities of all kinds must be sharply differentiated from proposals for merely widening the margins within which dealings are permitted. Unless the centre point is itself allowed to vary, the exchange rate will not be able to act as a regulator. The weak currencies would soon become wedged against their lower support points and the strong currencies against their upper points; we would then be back with fixed exchange rates.

Sliding parities could only be successfully inaugurated at a time when the starting parities were approximately correct. Otherwise the market would distrust the ability of national governments to limit exchange rate movements to the announced amount, and small interest variations would no longer be enough to counteract 'hot money' movements. This argument suggests that the early part of 1970 – after German revaluation, and when the British devaluation was showing signs of success – would have been an excellent time to inaugurate such a system. But as in the case of floating rates proper, it is just on such occasions that governments feel that existing policies are working and least feel the need for making experiments.

The practical differences between the market and discretionary variants of the slowly moving parity are not likely to be great. The permitted range of movement under the former will not be large enough to allow the exchange rate to balance the demand and supply for foreign exchange. In the short term, governments will have to use traditional weapons such as interest rate policies, overseas borrowing and lending operations, and general demand regulators; and with much less prospect of dramatic revaluations or devaluations such policies would influence the foreign exchange market very heavily. Sometimes the influence could be perverse. For example, if a creditor country tried to offset a current surplus by encouraging outward capital flows and slightly overdid it, the exchange rate could depreciate instead of appreciate. Once severe limits are imposed on exchange rate movements, central banks and Finance Ministers are bound to exercise a predominant influence in any case. The main argument for the market variant is that it would give private operators experience in operating with daily fluctuations in the parity, which would come in useful if the transition were ever made to genuinely floating rates.

Much of the discussion in the preceding pages about official intervention under floating rates is also relevant to slowly moving parities; but there are some issues worth treating separately.[28]

Might not a 2–3 per cent slide be too slow for cases of serious disequilibrium ?

Yes. A slowly moving rate would not have answered the needs of a country such as France in May 1968, where a 15 per cent general wage increase was suddenly conceded. In such cases a straight devaluation or period of floating would still have been required. Unlike floating rates, sliding parities cannot provide a system for all seasons. But by allowing gradual adjustment in more normal cases (of which Britain in the 1960s would have been an example), they would reduce enormously the number of full-scale parity changes required.

How would one prevent attempts by countries to steal a march on each other by competitive downward slides?

The answer is identical with that given on pp. 75-6 about the likelihood of preventing exchange rate wars under a regime of floating, but managed, rates. It is difficult to see why it should be more difficult to obtain international agreement to very small relative changes, which can be reversed if they are mistaken, than to large jumps such as the sterling, franc or mark moves of recent years. Indeed the Bundesbank could probably have persuaded the German Government to make small upward changes in the mark at a much earlier date, if these had been part of a series of routine technical decisions. In the last resort, however, a country that refused to allow deficit currencies to move down against it would end up holding a vast foreign exchange hoard and giving away its products for nothing.

Countries will only have incompatible exchange rate objectives if they have seriously incompatible balance of payments objectives. Apart from depression situations of the inter-war type, this would only happen if there were a general shortage of reserves, and surplus countries were so keen to add to their store that they were not prepared to allow deficit countries to move into balance. The launching of the new I.M.F. Drawing Rights should reduce the risks of such a situation, by allowing all countries to add simultaneously to their reserves. Progress with the 'adjustment' and 'liquidity' problems, so far from being alternatives, are interrelated (except in the alas unlikely world of freely floating rates without any sort of official intervention.)

How about the dollar? It cannot slide for the reasons you have yourself described.

So long as other currencies are managed in relation to the dollar, and the U.S.A. accepts the situation, this is true. Deficit countries would slide downwards in relation to the dollar, and surplus countries could choose whether to accumulate dollars or climb upwards.

Suppose countries in potential payments difficulties slide downwards against the dollar, and no one creeps upwards. Is there not a danger of the dollar emerging overvalued at the end of it all?

The situation postulated in the question implies a state of affairs in which the rest of the world is increasing its (official settlements) surplus against the U.S.A. But if this happens, simple arithmetic suggests that the likelihood of any individual currency in the rest of the world needing to depreciate will lessen; and the stronger countries will be accumulating larger and larger surpluses which would be holding back the living standards of their own inhabitants. Eventually there would be a reversal of fashions, with downward parity movements becoming a rarity and upward movement more frequent.

The above paragraph assumes that surplus countries would either not ask to have their official dollar balances converted into gold, or would have their requests refused. There is in fact great reluctance on either side of the Atlantic to precipitate a showdown over gold conversion, which would expose the 'official' $35 gold price for the convention that it is. Once a gold embargo were imposed, the dollar would of course be floating against gold. Other countries could tie their currencies to either the dollar or gold, or neither, but not to both. The central point to grasp among all these permutations and combinations is that trade and payments depend on the correct adjustment of currencies to each other; the price of currencies against gold is of little direct conern to the manufacturer of trader, however exciting the newspaper headlines on the subject.

Out of consideration for the dollar, as well as for anti-inflationary reasons, the I.M.F. is likely to look with more favour – or less disfavour – on upward than downward movement in any schemes for limited flexibility. Continental concern to fight off 'imported inflation' will also tilt the balance in this direction. The U.S. Council of Economic Advisers is particularly interested in 'presumptive rules' which would make it difficult for countries to move downwards without objective evidence of deficit in their external payments. These would basically be 'rules of the game' to be added to those that already govern the 'multilateral surveillance' undertaken in bodies such as Working Party Three.

As interest rates would have to be higher in deficit countries, by approximately the extent of the expected currency depreciation, does this not deprive countries of the use of interest rate policy for domestic stabilisation purposes?

This objection depends on the myth that countries, especially those like Britain with active international money markets, have freedom to decide their own interest rate policy under a 'fixed exchange rate'. To prevent a run on its currency such a country has in any case to offer interest rates sufficiently high to offset the devaluation risk. Under the present system, interest rates need to be more volatile – and much higher in periods of currency suspicion – than they would be if payments corrections were normally made by gradual parity adjustments.

A country whose currency seemed likely to crawl consistently downwards over several years would obviously need higher *nominal* interest rates than other countries. If this prospect were due to a faster rate of inflation, the *real* interest rate after taking price changes into account would not be specially high. But even if the prospect of gradual depreciation reflected non-price factors, such as an increasing defence burden, or a growing lack of competitiveness in design or delivery dates, the interest argument is helpful rather than embarrassing to the reformer. In all such situations, domestic spending would have to rise slightly more slowly than otherwise, and a greater volume of resources devoted to exports or import substitution; and an incentive to encourage people to save more and spend less would be helpful. If a country in this position tries to keep out of deficit under a fixed exchange rate, it will have – even more than under a moving rate – to restrict the growth of its money supply, and this too will push interest rates upwards.

The interest rate objection, like so many others, boils down either to a reluctance by countries to pay their way overseas altogether, or to wishful thinking by those who, despite all past experience, think that they can concern themselves with 'fine-tuning' domestically irrespective of the balance of payments.

Is any form of flexible rate compatible with British membership of the E.E.C.? Permanently fixed exchange rates have long been an objective of the Brussels Commission. Although the French and German parity changes represent a defeat for this objective, the Ministerial Council of the E.E.C., at their meeting at Luxembourg on 6 October 1969, set down in their recorded summary: 'They are of the opinion that in the longer run a system of fluctuating exchange rates is not compatible with the Common Market; they therefore insisted on the importance that the German measures should be applied only for the shortest possible time and that the German Government should take a definitive decision on the parity as soon as possible.'

This objection applies only to floating rates as such, and not to the small discretionary movements envisaged under some of the compromise schemes. But it is convenient to discuss the whole subject here.

1. We are not yet in the E.E.C. For nearly a decade governments have behaved as if we were on the verge of joining, and experience suggests that it would be foolhardy to take membership for granted. Moreover, a British move now, even to a fully floating rate, would do little to diminish the prospects of eventual membership. On the contrary, the nearer the exchange rate is to the equilibrium rate on the eve of joining, the easier will be the transition for both sides.

2. Membership is likely to impose a foreign exchange burden on the U.K. The great difficulty from a policy point of view is that its size will be largely a matter of guesswork, whatever the 'terms'. On the eve of membership a U.K. Government will thus be more than usually uncertain about the underlying movement of the balance of payments in the years ahead. Even if a jump to a new fixed sterling parity change were politically acceptable, the Treasury would not know whether to propose one, and if so, of what size. The Governor of the Bank of Italy, Signor Carli, in a distinguished report to the Monnet Action Committee for the United States of Europe,[29] has suggested that the

adoption of slowly moving parities with the enlarged E.E.C. would overcome these difficulties during the transitional period.

3. There is no economic reason why floating parities should be incompatible even with the Common Agricultural Policy. The translation of unit of account prices (effectively dollars) into fluctuating national units is a simple computer job. As Graham Hallett has shown,[30] the tensions arise not from exchange rate movements as such, but from divergent movements in the productivity gap between agriculture and industry in different countries. Imagine that productivity in German industry and agriculture rose at the same pace. If wages rose less than in other countries or productivity more, appreciation might still have been necessary. But the fall in agricultural prices, measured in D-marks, would have been compensated for by a favourable movement in German farm costs relative to those of other countries. The trouble arises when German industrial productivity rises more quickly than agricultural, in a way that is not paralleled in other Community members. In this situation an exchange rate which secures overall equilibrium, and can be borne by German industry, will harm the farmers. An exchange rate that keeps the farmers happy will, however, result in a chronic German surplus. The dilemma reflects 'real' rather than monetary divergences and would emerge sooner or later whatever the currency regime.

Sr Carli's recommendation of small discretionary changes to be announced every month or quarter, and not to exceed 2 per cent per annum, was meant to apply not merely to the U.K. in a transitional period, but to the whole Community, until policies are so harmonised that these changes are unnecessary. The effects of such a system on the Common Agricultural Policy will be no different in kind, and smaller in degree, than those arising from normal lump-sum revaluations or devaluations. Indeed nothing could have been more disruptive than the large premia and discounts which prevailed in forward markets when the mark and franc rates were distrusted, and which enabled German merchants to buy French grain for future delivery at far below the price which German farmers were receiving.

4. *The arguments for British membership of the E.E.C. are stronger, not weaker, if a flexible view is taken of exchange rates.* According to the conventional view, the burden of British membership consists (*a*) of the initial transfer across the exchanges to finance the C.A.P., (*b*) any other net foreign exchange outflow, e.g. to finance British investment in Europe, and (*c*) the secondary effects on the balance of payments of

higher wages, induced by higher food prices. In fact only the first of these need be a real burden. The secondary effects mentioned under (*c*) represent numbers on pieces of paper, while any increase in overseas investment under (*b*) reflects an opportunity to raise the return on British capital and improve our future terms of trade.

There may be some logic in what you are saying. But has not the recent mood in the E.E.C. been running strongly in the other direction? The Six are working on plans for 'monetary union'. These would provide inter alia *for the pooling of some reserves, a system of Community 'swaps', common guidelines on credit, and would aim to rule out all parity changes within the E.E.C. by the end of the decade.*

The Common Market Commission has been pushing such ideas as a way of increasing its role in monetary matters, which – up to 1970 – was hard to discern. It has been supported in particular by the Belgian and French Governments – in the latter case mainly as a tactical move in the manœuvring over the agricultural finance arrangements. (There can be few countries in Western Europe that have changed their exchange rate more than France.) British official circles are sceptical of the moves. But they think it prudent not to oppose them in public while the U.K. is seeking admission to the E.E.C.

The problems involved in creating larger currency areas have been discussed on pp. 71–5. The attempt to freeze rates within the E.E.C. (coming interestingly enough in the wake of major German and French parity changes) is almost certain to fail. Movements of prices, costs and competitive conditions, even among countries of the present Six, have often been closer to those of third countries than to those of fellow E.E.C. members. Germany has had to revalue twice in the last nine years and France has had to devalue twice in the last twelve. Thus both the mark and the franc were nearer to the dollar in their movements than either was to the other. If the parity changes in these two currencies had been prevented, Germany would have had to tolerate excessive inflation and France excessive unemployment – or alternatively impose all sorts of open and hidden controls on trade and payments.

The creation of the E.E.C. and its prospective enlargement increase the sensitivity of each member country's balance of payments to small relative differences in costs and prices, delivery dates and other aspects of competitive performance. Until the area becomes an effective economic union, the need for an adjustment mechanism is therefore actually increased. A workable economic union would not only require an effective co-ordination of fiscal and monetary policy throughout the Community, which we have yet to see in practice, but it would also require regional aid on a massive scale. Otherwise the less favoured countries would have all the disadvantages that Scotland, Northern Ireland and Wales have in not being able to devalue against England, but none of the fiscal and other regional aid they receive as a substitute.

An economic union would thus require a European Government (which could be of a confederal kind) whether labelled as such or not. But even this might not be enough. For there may be no feasible pattern of financial policies which would secure an acceptable behaviour of unemployment and price levels throughout the E.E.C. area. In the past few years a degree of financial toughness in France, sufficient to have preserved external equilibrium without parity changes, would have involved an unacceptably high degree of unemployment; and in Germany it would have involved needless inflation. A grand European co-ordinator would have had to face the fact that the more he helped the Germans to avoid inflation, the worse French unemployment would be, and the more he helped the French to avoid unnecessary unemployment, the worse German inflation would be. It will take many years before reactions of employers and unions and general public psychology become similar enough throughout Western Europe for a single currency area to be on the cards. An attempt to freeze parities before such conditions exist could backfire badly and leave behind a trail of trade restrictions and sudden devaluations which would jeopardise the gains already achieved within the Community. The basic mistake made by the Brussels Commission and its supporters has been to confuse the *results* of a far-reaching economic union with the *means* of achieving it, a mistake that could actually retard the final goal.

If membership of the E.E.C. were really to debar all exchange rate changes, this would be a serious argument against Britain joining, especially as the other arguments are so finely balanced. But there is no such prospect. Recent events have shown the impossibility of barring them. Despite all the talk in Brussels, it is extremely difficult to imagine our prospective E.E.C. partners preventing us from moving or revaluing by small amounts over a period on the grounds that big disturbing jumps were preferable. Freedom to make small and gradual parity adjustments during the transitional period should be treated as a vital British interest in the coming negotiations.

An attitude of watching on the sidelines in the hope (*a*) that we will not have to adjust our rate, or (*b*) that if we do we will face the problem when it arrives, is a dubious policy. It might one day dawn on politicians and officials that the U.K. has suffered more than any other country from the lack of exchange rate flexibility in the past, that the need for such flexibility will be even greater if we join the E.E.C., and that there is some advantage in expressing a view early rather than late. A suppliant posture does not earn respect and has not served us well in previous discussions with the E.E.C. It is unfortunate that the currency issue has been obscured by the almost exclusive preoccupation with agriculture that has characterised the European debate in Britain.

You have spoken so far in terms of what might be possible or desirable. But you have also explained some of the deep-seated reasons why governments are not inclined to move to flexibility. How likely do you think a change in the system is in practice?

Exchange rate flexibility has been studied by the staff of the I.M.F. This was arranged at the Fund's annual meeting in the autumn of 1969. The fact that such studies could be arranged, and openly discussed, represents a great step forward compared with the position only a few years ago when the whole subject was taboo. Although the U.S. has inhibitions about downward flexibility, for the reasons already explained, there is strong support for the idea of gradual upward movement in the parities of creditor countries. The U.S. Council of Economic Advisers strongly advocates flexibility and it has many supporters within the U.S. Treasury and even among the Federal Reserve Governors. The coolness of Secretary of the Treasury Kennedy at the 1969 I.M.F. meeting was more a tactical move than a defeat for this school. On the Continent there is, despite the Brussels development, support for slowly moving parities on a discretionary basis in the German, Italian and the Netherlands' central banks and also in the German Economics Ministry.

The I.M.F. report (not yet ready at the time of going to press) is likely for diplomatic reasons (and to avoid disturbing markets) to be written in as low a key as possible and to underplay rather than overplay any changes suggested. Nevertheless, there is a fair chance that there will be a mention of circumstances in which more flexibility would be acceptable for surplus countries, and just possibly – and with many more qualifications – for deficit countries too. If this accolade of respectability is granted, it would be much easier for official advocates of flexibility in the various national centres to make headway within their governments. One can visualise a number of distinct ways in which increased flexibility might occur:

(1) Some form of gradually moving rate may be adopted during the transitional period while the U.K. is entering the E.E.C. There will then of course be opportunity for argument about how transitional the parity arrangements should really be.

(2) One or other surplus country anxious to avoid importing inflation might announce an upward moving rate on a discretionary basis.

(3) Countries may continue with fixed rate parity changes, but make such changes smaller, more frequent and more normal occurrences. If this should happen, transitional periods of floating rates, similar to the German experiment last autumn, but less circumscribed, would probably become a feature of the currency landscape.

(4) If the U.S. were to get into serious payments difficulties, and unwilling official holders of dollars were formally or informally refused permission to convert into gold, some of them might choose to sell their dollars on the market and thus establish a floating rate between their own currencies and the dollar.

The odds are against any one of these possibilities taken separately. But added together the chances are more than 50 per cent that, by one or other of these routes, the world will reach a more flexible system. Progress here, as in other matters, cannot, however, be taken for granted, and flexibility is always a matter of degree. It will not do therefore simply to wait on events.

Conclusion

Some of the preceding pages have had to delve into complicated issues. This makes it all the more important to separate the issue of principle from the technical questions. The point of principle is that exchange rate changes should be used as a normal method of international adjustment, and that we should never again be prepared to make the preservation of an overvalued parity the principle aim of British Governments. This would entail the end of the obsession with earning or saving foreign exchange; £1 of currency would be treated of equal value whether earned in sterling, dollars or marks, no more, no less.

How to reach such a situation is a practical matter. I have argued in earlier chapters that it is most unlikely to be reached under the present system of normally fixed, but in the last resort adjustable, exchange rates. The choice of which type of flexibility to adopt is partly a technical question and partly a matter of political judgment about the reaction of governments in different circumstances. My own preference is for floating rates, as under any of the compromise schemes there would be a danger of governments not exercising, out of wishful thinking, their option of moving the rate by the permitted annual amount until a substantial overvaluation was clear. I also think for reasons explained at the end of the Appendix that a fully floating rate would at this particular moment be the least inflationary system. But half a loaf is better than no bread; and any system under which exchange rates could move without a vast political upheaval would be a great step forward.

If Richard Cobden were alive today he would be likely to crusade against the present system of reluctant exchange rate adjustment, which presents the same barriers to the sensible use of resources and international amity as the Corn Laws did in the first half of the nineteenth century. The supporters of 'fixed rates' are required to show not merely that there are difficulties and dangers in flexibility. So there are in every policy including the present. They have to show that the dangers of flexibility are so great as to be worth all the far-reaching damage to the cause of rationality, prosperity, freedom, the rule of law and a healthy national psychology discussed in the preceding pages.

Although consultation and co-operation with other national authorities would be necessary, a shift to a flexible rate could be made by Britain unilaterally and without bad-neighbourliness. A great prize is waiting for any British Government that changes the rules of the game so that we no longer need to distort all our other policies for balance of payments reasons, and can concentrate instead on making the best use of our resources, uninhibited by self-created problems. The rest of us can bring forward this happy day by refusing to be taken in on any future occasion by official propaganda about the balance of payments. There is no patriotic duty to help resolve a pseudo-problem created by pretending that the pound is worth something slightly different from what it really is.

Appendix: Inflation, Employment and Growth

Advocates of flexible rates are always suspected of being advocates of inflation, or at least excessively tolerant in their attitude to it; this suspicion often lies at the heart of at least one set of objections. It therefore seems worth while to append a personal summary of the state of the debate on demand management and economic growth. Since this is not the primary object of the present book, the assessments below will be given as a bold summary, with no attempt to set out the supporting arguments.

If it were true that inflation helped growth, and the growth were not just of the statistical Gross National Product but, after allowing for all adverse side-effects, contributed to welfare; and if this additional growth were large enought to outweigh any adverse social or political implications of the extra inflation, then one should be prepared to tolerate inflation up to the point where this ceased to be true. So should any logical man of goodwill.

Anti-inflationists should concentrate their attacks on the many conditional clauses in the above statement; if these are taken seriously, they will rarely lead to the support of an inflationary policy. Their frequent failure to focus their attacks in this way in the past, and their habit of talking as if the price index, and *a fortiori* the exchange rate, were an independent objective of policy rather than a means, certainly accounted for the flirtation of the younger generation of economic writers with inflationary policies for so long a period.

There were very few 'expansionist' writers who actually believed that rising prices *per se* help growth. But some did believe that economic policies which aimed at high and rising levels of demand did stimulate growth. They realised that such policies carried a greater risk of inflation, which they thought had to be accepted.

Such a view is no longer tenable in the light of both recent theory and recent evidence. In fact the authorities have much less influence on the level of real demand of employment and capacity utilisation than much of the discussion in the 1960s assumed. Faith in the ability of the authorities to regulate the pressure of demand on resources and obtain a given optimum unemployment percentage was excessive both among the 'Paish school of thought' and their expansionist critics.

In the long run an increase in monetary demand above that consistent with approximate price stability has its overwhelming effect on the level of prices and very little on output and employment. If monetary demand is boosted from, say, a level consistent with a $2\frac{1}{2}$ per cent increase in the price index to one consistent with a stable non-accelerating 6 per cent increase, there will initially be an increase n em ployment and 'real' business activity. But the level of employment will afterwards gradually slip back to one no higher than we would have obtained if we had stuck to a $2\frac{1}{2}$ per cent rate of price inflation all along. This would be so even in a closed economy with no balance of payments constraint.

If the above is accepted as at least provisionally true, then by Occam's Razor many of the other arguments are irrelevant; and we do not need to discuss the advantages of high-demand policies in promoting labour-saving investment, or low-demand policies in promoting a more competitive environment. This is because the authorities have not more than a temporary power to bring about either state of affairs. It is worth being cautious about rates of inflation in roughly the $0 - 2\frac{1}{2}$ per cent per annum range. Quality changes, index number difficulties, and an irreducible minimum level of money illusion could make it both painful and unnecessary to insist on a zero rate of measured price increases. But arguments within this range are not at present of practical relevance, and many of the most convinced opponents of inflation would happily settle for anywhere within the $0 - 2\frac{1}{2}$ per cent price range as a vast improvement on anything that has been known in the post-war period.

There are, nevertheless, some remaining grounds for being cautious about the uninhibited pursuit of deflationary demand policies:

1. The economic system is extremely resistant to downward changes in the general price level.

2. It is also resistant to any but the most gradual reduction in any given rate of inflation once it has been firmly established and built into the pattern of expectations, interest rates, and wage and price behaviour.

Attempts to disregard the above points can lead to unemployment that is transient only in some extremely long-run 'when we're all dead' sense. In practice such downward pressure is likely to be resisted and not taken very far by the authorities, and instead policy diverted into direct controls of various kinds, open and suppressed.

3. Unnecessary irregularities in the pace of expansion of monetary demand – i.e. avoidable 'stop – go' – are harmful to genuine growth. The extent of this harm is controversial and has never been quantified. But its amount would probably reflect the psychological atmosphere of the time. If a check to demand were believed, whether logically or not, to be due to a balance of payments constraint which – given a fixed exchange rate – might check the permissible expansion of demand for a long time to come, the effect on investment could be serious and worse than that of Continental-type squeezes primarily imposed to check domestic inflation.

4. The joint effect of the above three points is that a rational citizen should oppose any attempt to bring about a quick and drastic reduction in the growth of monetary demand, e.g. from that consistent with a 6 per cent inflation rate to that consistent with a 2 per cent one, for this would lead to a very long transitional stage involving considerable dangers of unemployment and recession. He would, on the other hand, favour early action to curb an inflationary boom while there is still time. In all probability there would be less danger of inflationary booms getting out of hand, if instead of relying solely on the ability of the authorities to identify them in time, there were also long-run rules limiting the permissible deficit on a full employment budget and the annual growth of the money supply. This, however, is a separate argument.

If, however, an inflationary movement were not tackled in time and the economy were set on a course of rapidly rising prices, the best course would be to avoid a sudden or severe check to the growth of demand, but to reduce slightly the rate of inflation, year by year, until eventually price increases are back within the 0 – $2\frac{1}{2}$ per cent per annum bracker. Such a course, however, requires strong nerves and patience.

The residual difference of opinion between the above and the British economic establishment comes down to a difference over behaviour in crisis years such as 1957, 1961 and 1966. At such times the economy has had to be hit on the head when the peak of the boom had already been passed, and this could truly be blamed on the failure to act in good time. The conventional view might regard this as unfortunate but inevitable; on the other hand, those who follow the argument presented above, would argue for 'gradualist' courses designed to squeeze inflationary forces out of the economy over a fairly long period.

This latter is the view not just of 'Left-wing' Keynesians, but even more of Professor Milton Friedman and the monetarist school normally regarded as 'extreme Right'. The gradualist approach could even be the less inflationary one when viewed in proper perspective. For it is very often the shock effects of belated deflationary action that create political concern over unemployment and an eventual reversal of policy in a highly inflationary direction. This is what, after all, happened after all the crisis episodes mentioned above.

Under a fully floating exchange rate there would be no external constraint on the rate of inflation, and this would force politicians, officials and commentators to give much more thought to the real domestic costs of rapidly rising prices. Those concerned with public affairs have become so accustomed to supposing that adverse balance of payments consequences are the only argument against inflation that they have paid very little attention to the more fundamental arguments for more stable prices. Ten or fifteen years ago there was less experience of the effects of rising prices, or evidence of the dangers of acceleration, and more room for wishful thinking about the effects of inflation in stimulating growth. If the balance of payments pretext were dropped and the price-level policy considered on its merits, the result could well be a good deal less inflation than would be otherwise likely.

Notes and References

1. E. J. Mishan, *The Cost of Economic Growth* (Staples Press, 1967; Penguin Books, 1969) chap. 2.

2. Harry Johnson, 'The Case for Flexible Exchange Rates', in Hobart Paper No. 46, *U.K. and Floating Rates* (Institute of Economic Affairs, 1969) is much the best short statement of the argument. An opposing point of view is presented by Mr John Nash in 'U.K. Policy and International Monetary Reform' in the same Paper. Another I.E.A. Paper discussing the subject as part of a wide canvas is Gottfried Haberler, *Money in the International Economy*, Hobart Paper No. 31, 2nd ed. (1969).

The classic statement of the case for floating rates has been put forward by Professor Milton Friedman. The earliest, fullest and probably still the best version is 'The Case for Flexible Rates'. This can be found in *Essays in Positive Economics* (Chicago, 1953). An abbreviated version is reprinted in *Readings in International Economics*, ed. R. E. Caves and H. G. Johnson (1968). Later versions can be found in *Capitalism and Freedom* (Chicago, 1962) and *Dollars and Deficits* (New York, 1968).

Readers who want a greater quantity of information and analysis than is possible in essay form are particularly referred to Leland B. Yeager, *International Monetary Relations: Theory, History and Policy* (New York, 1966). This monumental 500-page work, which seems to be hardly known in policy-making circles in this country, analyses exhaustively contentious issues such as elasticity pessimism, inflationary repercussions, speculation, official intervention and exchange risk and international trade. The historical section starts with the period *prior* to the establishment of the late-nineteenth-century international gold standard, and ends with contemporary problems of the dollar, sterling, the European currencies, gold and the I.M.F. This section is particularly noteworthy for the criticism it makes of Ragner Nurkse's study, *International Currency Experiences* (League of Nations, 1944), which is the source of manyof the supposed anti-flexibility 'lessons' of inter-war experience.

Another important recent book is Egon Sohmen, *Flexible Exchange Rates*, 2nd ed. (Chicago, 1969). Although primarily addressed to economists, it does deal with many of the objections put forward in City and business circles; the last chapter in particular should be comprehensible to the layman with a special interest in the subject.

3. 'Problems of Balance of Payments Adjustment in the Modern World', in *Essays in Money and Banking in Honour of R. S. Sayers* (Oxford, 1968).

4. For a fuller account and analysis of this episode, see Samuel Brittan, *Steering the Economy* (Penguin Books, 1970) chap. 9.

5. See, for instance, Brittan, *ibid.*, pt. II.

6. The argument here is identical with that about the effects of relying on unaided deflation without devaluation to restore balance when a currency is overvalued. This is discussed, with illustrative calculations in relation to the 1967 British devaluation, in *ibid.* (at the beginning of chap. 9 in the Penguin edition and chap. 11 in the hard-back version).

7. *Britain's Economic Prospects.* (Washington and London, 1968) 155.

8. For detailed evidence to support this assertion, see B. Balassa, 'The Purchasing Power Doctrine: A Reappraisal', in *International Finance*, ed. R. N. Cooper (Penguin Books, 1969). For recent years consult the regular table 'Industrial Countries. Consumer Prices' in any recent issue of the *National Institute Economic Review*. The figures have to be adjusted for parity changes.

9. *Britain's Economic Prospects*, chap. 4.

10. *A Study of United Kingdom Imports* (Cambridge, 1963) pp. 43, 100.

11. An element of judgment is required because we do not know what the terms of trade would have been without devaluation. The difficulty is that there is no index for services. The terms of trade of services are unlikely to have deteriorated as much here, because a good many service items, such as shipping or insurance, are geared to international prices, and their sterling equivalents would have gone up in proportion to the devaluation. If the index is applied only to goods, the deterioration would have cost about £200 million in 1968. If it is applied to services as well, the cost would have been just under £270 million.

12. Information supplied by Professor Douglas Hague.

13. Para. 37.

14. *Britain in the World*, paras. 23, 37, 45

15. *Capitalism and Freedom*, p. 69.

16. Sohmen, *Flexible Exchange Rates*, p. 201.

17. See Richard Caves and G. L. Reuber, *Canadian Economic Policy and the Impact of International Capital Flows* (Toronto, 1969) and, for a more technical analysis, their *Capital Transfer and Economic Policy: Canada, 1951-62* (Harvard, 1970).

18. *International Currency Experience* (League of Nations, 1944).

19. A succinct but devastating attack on Nurkse's analytical methods can be found in Friedman's *Essays in Positive Economics*, A detailed alternative interpretation of the relevant episodes can be found in Yeager, *International Monetary Relations*, chaps. 10, 15, 16 and 17.

20. Oxford, 1944.

21. For further details of these historical episodes and references to primary sources, see Yeager, *International Monetary Relations*, chaps. 12 and 14. See also his paper on 'Fluctuating Exchange Rates in the nineteenth century: The Experiences of Austria and Russia', in *Monetary Problems of the International Economy*, ed. R. A. Mundell and A. K. Swobida (Chicago, 1969).

22. Professor Sohmen has, however, provided interesting arguments for supposing that even short-term monetary policy would be much more effective under floating than under fixed rates, in *Flexible Exchange Rates*, chap. 5. A less technical summary of the argument is given in chap. 7, section 6.

23. The figures cited are based on the concepts used by Professor A. A. Walters in *Money in Boom and Slump*, Hobart Paper 44 (1969) pp. 22–30.

24 *The Reform of Sterling*, Princeton Essays in International Finance, No. 77 (Princeton, 1970).

25. Sohmen, *Flexible Exchange Rates*, chap. 7, section 2.

26. See *A Theory of Economic History* (Oxford, 1969) chaps. 5 and 6.

27. See Herbert Grubel in *Monetary Problems of the International Economy*, p. 269, and subsequent comment and recorded discussion.

28. For a more detailed discussion of the issues raised by slowly moving parities, see J. H. Williamson, *The Crawling Peg*, Essays in International Finance, No. 50 (Princeton, 1965) and subsequent essays in the Princeton series. See also the *Annual Report of the Council of Economic Advisers* (Washington, 1970).

29. *Problems of British Entry* (Chatham House and P.E.P., 1969).

30. The Problem of Agriculture in a European Economic Union, *Journal of Agricultural Economics*, vol. xx, no. 3 (1969).

Index